INSTANT CASHFLOW

**Action
International**

Business Coaching

Other Books in the Instant Success Series

INSTANT CASHFLOW

BRADLEY J. SUGARS

McGraw-Hill

New York   Chicago   San Francisco   Lisbon   London
Madrid   Mexico City   Milan   New Delhi   San Juan
Seoul   Singapore   Sydney   Toronto

1 2 3 4 5 6 7 8 9 0   FGR/FGR   0 9 8 7 6 5

ISBN 0-07-146659-2

This publication is designed to provide accurate and authoritative information in regard to the subject matter covered. It is sold with the understanding that neither the author nor the publisher is engaged in rendering legal, accounting, or other professional service. If legal advice or other expert assistance is required, the services of a competent professional person should be sought.
—From a Declaration of Principles jointly adopted by Committee of the American Bar Association and a Committee of Publishers.

McGraw-Hill books are available at special quantity discounts to use as premiums and sales promotions, or for use in corporate training programs. For more information, please write to the Director of Special Sales, McGraw-Hill Professional, Two Penn Plaza, New York, NY 10121-2298. Or contact your local bookstore.

Library of Congress Cataloging-in-Publication Data

Sugars, Bradley J.
    Instant cashflow / Bradley J. Sugars.—1st ed.
        p.   cm.
    ISBN 0-07-146659-2 (pbk. : alk. paper)
    1. Cash management.   2. Cash flow.   3. Marketing—
Management.   4. Small business—Management.   I. Title.
    HG4028.C45S84 2006
658.8—dc22   2005054502

To Mom and Dad.
You always knew the right thing to say.

▌Contents

▌ Acknowledgments

Neither a book, nor the knowledge you acquire to write it, come without the efforts of a group of people. I'd really like to thank my editor Christian Dige for his ability to make my writing worthy of publishing, and my team at Action International.

Thanks also to Action International's team of business coaches.

A big thanks goes to my biggest supporters, you, my clients whose success has built my success, whose support has helped us build a dream, and whose questions have helped me learn a great deal about what it is I know.

Thanks to my teachers, Claude Hopkins, John Caples, Buckminster Fuller, Jim Rohn, Mardi Palmer, Vicki Bailey, Phillip Barham, Mark Tier, Tony Robbins, Murray Raphel, Paul Cunn, Jay Abraham, Michael Gerber, Blair Singer, Dolf deRoos, John Burley, and all of the teachers who's books, tapes, and seminars have meant so much in guiding me to business success.

Most of all I'd like to thank my parents. My dad for his dry humor and ability to point out the obvious, even when noone else can see what needs to be done. My mom for her love, care and support no matter what decisions I made. And, to my brothers for their ability to challenge me in ways I never dreamed of.

And to Jennifer. Your love and support mean more to me than you'll ever know. Thank you for everything.

∎ Introduction

Over the years I've helped thousands of businesses reach, and then exceed, their potential. I've helped thousands of business owners make their dreams come true. In each and every instance it's been achieved by applying a set of core principles that anyone can use. And these principles will very quickly make your business flourish, even when times are bad.

This is a book about getting results above and beyond the ordinary, and yet it's a simple book. You'll be literally amazed at the simplicity with which you'll be able to work and add many tens of thousands, hundreds of thousands, or even tens of millions to your turnover and profit just by finding and working on what I call your business *gold mines*.

It doesn't matter whether you sell paper clips or airplanes, the ideas and stories you're about to be exposed to will revolutionize the way you view, and practice, your profession. So get ready for a radical transformation.

So, what makes me an expert? Where do I get off telling people how to run their businesses? I know it's a hackneyed term, but the runs are on the board.

From running more than a dozen of my own companies to listening to a bunch of business masters, watching what people do right, wrong, and indifferently, reading every piece of material available, and then, analyzing, testing and measuring, working with thousands of clients, and taking my own businesses global, I've managed to pinpoint the ways to catapult your bottom line.

That was the first step. The second and much more difficult step was putting it in terms that everyone can understand. Having used the knowledge for great personal reward, I now want to spread the message through this book.

This means distilling the information so you can easily grasp it. And that's what this book is all about. It's about people like you taking my knowledge, having me coach you, applying it to your own business, and then enjoying the same rewards that I have.

I know you can do it—I've literally seen it done thousands of times.

Making It Easy to Understand

Instant Cashflow is separated into four parts. I've done this in an attempt to relay all the information in such a way that you'll not only absorb the message but also see how effective it is when implemented. And that's the key. It's no good having hundreds of great ideas if you do nothing with them.

That's why we begin with the attitude part of growing a business.

Part 1—Preparing the Mind

This is titled "Think Like I Think" and it's a checklist of your mental approach to business. Without an open mind and the right attitude, you might as well just go back to a paycheck-to-paycheck existence working for someone else. You must be willing to change the way you think, so you can change the things you do, so you can improve the results you're getting. Remember the saying that goes something like this: "To do the same thing over and over again, and expect a different result, is the definition of insanity."

If you haven't got an open mind that's prepared for a few adjustments, return this book immediately to wherever you bought it and get a refund, or exchange it for a novel. Opening your mind is vital.

After opening up your mind, we get into the really juicy stuff that is guaranteed to boost your profits.

Part 2—How to Become a Marketing Genius

The second section about understanding marketing lays bare the secrets that have made me millions. Actually, I use the term *secrets* a little loosely. It's more about common sense. But as we all know common sense is far from common.

For those new to marketing, it will get you off on the right foot. For those who've been around a while, it will mean a massive realignment of your marketing strategy. Either way it will unlock the most important business principals known to man.

Learn how to market and the world is yours. Yet it amazes me how many people blindly spend money hand over fist on their marketing without ever reviewing the results. They limit themselves to a few basic areas—like a weekly ad in the local newspaper—without every asking themselves, "Is this really the best medium? Could I get a better return on the investment by writing a better ad?"

If you belong to this group, the good news is you're not alone. Most people do it. But by the end of this book you won't be taking any more chances with your marketing. You'll know exactly what will work best, and importantly, you'll be constantly testing and measuring your results so not a cent is wasted.

Part 3—My Mechanic and the Business Chassis

The third section of the book revolves around my mechanic. That's right, Charlie, my mechanic.

This chapter will change the way you think about the world of making money. What we're going to do is break down your business into the five different areas that constitute your profitability: the leads you can generate, the conversion rate of those leads into sales, the transaction rate of those customers—how many times they buy, the average dollar amount spent per sale, and then your margins.

This is what I call the Business Chassis and when grasped, it'll blow your mind. It will provide you with an infinitely simpler way of understanding the factors that make your business more profitable, and as a result you can do something constructive about it.

As previously mentioned, one of my biggest challenges was figuring out the best way to relay the message, because it literally sounds too good to be true. So instead of just explaining how it works, I thought I'd relay an encounter with Charlie, a small businessman with big dreams.

After a little pep talk about how all business revolves around the aforementioned Business Chassis, I could see Charlie was ready to do anything to improve his very promising, yet completely unfulfilled, enterprise. It was then that I decided to take Charlie on a little tour.

I took Charlie to all different kinds of businesses that had received and implemented my advice—a different business for each part of the chassis. They were actually making it happen, and I wanted Charlie to see their achievements firsthand. Not only for practical guidance but also for a dose of much-needed inspiration.

It's amazing how much more attainable something seems when you physically see it happening. Take the tour with Charlie and you'll see it for yourself.

It's a creative little story, but you'll clearly see how it's possible to transform your business and create instant cashflow.

Part 4—282 Tips to Make It Happen

Next, I've included 282 practical marketing and sales ideas that you can apply to your business right now. So, *no excuses*. And, I've included simple-to-understand and easy-to-use forms to assist you every step of the way.

You can't say, "Oh, that all sounds great in theory, but how do I actually make it happen?" It's all there with 282 real-life ways of putting the theory into *Action*.

As each enterprise presents a unique set of challenges, not all my suggestions will apply to your business. That's why I've included so many. This is a comprehensive guide detailing most of the techniques at your disposal to boost each part of the Business Chassis. From referral programs to TV advertising, it's all there with an explanation of how it works. By working through each part, noting which strategies apply to your business or which you'd like to try, and then completing the relevant form, you'll be developing your own instant marketing plan that will get your business pumping. That's right—by just reading this book and filling in the relevant forms, you will end up with an instant marketing plan that really works. I'd be amazed if you couldn't take away at least 25 ideas that will immediately start making your business more profitable. And better still, it might expose a few strategies that you are sinking money into as a complete waste of time.

These ideas have been collected over years by trial and error, testing and measuring, and exhaustive research. They are categorised into the five different areas of the Business Chassis, so you can target each area as a separate challenge.

And as you'll see, it only takes a 15 to 20 percent increase in each of the five main areas of your business to more than double your profits.

Can you do that? With what you're about to learn, of course you can!

I've even given each method a score out of five, based on my experiences. You'll also find some techniques I wouldn't recommend. That's done so you can pinpoint dollars spent on marketing that you might be flushing down the toilet.

Testing and Measuring

If you don't know where your customers come from, you're really stabbing around in the dark.

You'll have no real idea which marketing campaigns are working, how well your salespeople are doing, or even how much each sale is *costing* you.

Once you know these things, you'll have the power to make decisions, and good ones at that. You'll know which marketing campaigns to kill, which to improve, and which to spend more money on.

You'll also know where your key leverage point is, that is, the thing that you most need to improve. Perhaps your conversion rate is high but your leads are few. Maybe it's the other way around. Maybe you're doing well in both lead generation and conversion, but you're not selling enough high-priced items.

Once you know which area to work on, you can start making new, well-informed marketing decisions.

The journey towards extraordinary profits begins here.

Enjoy the ride—and good luck!

INSTANT CASHFLOW

Part 1

▐ Preparing the Mind

Think How I Think

Simple fact: How you think, what you know to be true, and what you believe to be true about how you do business is what brought you to where you are right now.

And as good, bad, or (as you'll soon learn) *interesting* your current position may be, if you want to get results like I get for my businesses and for my business coaching clients, then you'd better learn a new way of thinking, before you learn a new way of doing.

It's the way I think that's allowed me to discover and profit from the hundreds of sales, marketing, and business-building tools you'll find at the back of this book. So, let's start with the big ones.

Only the Responsible Will Thrive

Every day you see another poor lost soul whom the world has mistreated, pushed around, and left along the side of the road for dead. What a load of rubbish.

You'll never survive in business thinking like that, thinking that the world is in charge. It still amazes me the number of people who live their life from a *victim's* point of view. They'll blame anyone and everyone for their lot in life. And, if there's no one to blame, they'll either come up with an excuse or totally deny that anything's going wrong. If this is you, you've got to change, or you should go back and get a job. By the way, *job* is nothing more than an acronym for *Just over Broke*.

In the world of owning and running your own business, you know one thing for a fact, only *you* can change what's going on in your business. You can't blame your team members, your competition, the government, your mother-in-law, or anyone else, because when you point the finger at someone else, you've still got three of your own pointing back at you. Ever stopped and looked at that? Just try it, point at someone, and notice where the rest of your fingers point.

Only *you* can make a difference in your own life. No more blaming others, making excuses, or living in denial. What I call "playing below the line."

If you want to create amazing results in business, you've got to take total ownership, be held accountable for your results, and be totally responsible for your actions. What I call *playing above the line*. It's the only way what I teach you can ever work. So make the choice; agree with yourself right now that from now on you'll play above the line.

Life Is Meant to Be Full of Mistakes

The only reason I know more than most people is that I've made more mistakes than most people have. You've got to be willing to take some risks. You've got to be willing to fall down. You've got to be willing to participate 100 percent at all times.

Remember back to when you first learned to walk. How many shots at getting up and walking did you give yourself before you called it quits? Did your parents show you how to do it and then say, "Well you've fallen down 17 times, that's it. You'll never learn to walk. You'll be a crawler." Not likely.

You kept going until you found a way to get there. If one thing didn't work, you tried another. You pushed on until you reached your goal. Your will and determination didn't have this thing called *pride*, or *common sense* standing in the way. You'll need to remember this as you strive for sales, marketing, and cashflow success.

The only way you can lose is to stop trying, because every time you make an attempt, you learn another way not to do it. Commit to yourself. The only way you can fail is to not participate at 100 percent. Failure is only the failure to participate 100 percent.

What If It Was Just "Interesting?"

Have you ever had an argument, a really good one? You argued because you were right, and they were wrong. But from their point of view, the exact opposite was true; they were right and you were wrong. So, at that same point in time you were both right, and both wrong. What was different was your points of view.

And then, even though you'd argued until you were blue in the face to prove your point, a few days later you found out you were wrong. Ever had this happen?

In my world, instead of arguing, I live by the simple saying, "Isn't that interesting." When someone brings up a point I don't really agree with I just say, "Isn't that interesting."

Here's the basis for this entire position in life. For there to be up, there's down, left, there's right, and so on. If I have to prove myself right, I'm cutting off all possibility that there might be a better way. So, as you read, remember, you don't have to agree; just see it as interesting. And now it's possible that you'll learn a better way.

Business Is Fun!

If you're going to play the game of business, I will give you just three pieces of advice. First, learn the rules. Second, keep score *(both of these are covered in this book)* and third, have fun *(that will come as a result of reading and implementing the advice in this book)*. So many people treat business as a life and death struggle and then discover that that's exactly what it has become.

You go into business for whatever reason, but most of all, it's to give yourself a better lifestyle. More money, more time, more freedom, and then, if you're like most people, you let the whole thing suck you up and the game plays you, instead of your playing the game.

Give yourself a break; it's a game. Have some fun. Enjoy yourself. Always keep fun as one of your primary aims. In other words, if you're not enjoying what you're doing, either decide to start enjoying it, or get out.

How often do you hear of immensely wealthy people who lead miserable lives? Success comes in many forms, and it's important to remember that money isn't a panacea for happiness. It's imperative to keep some balance in your life, and this often means keeping your business in perspective.

It's not life or death, and the more you view it accordingly, the more success will come your way.

You Are Your Biggest Business Project

I was once taught by a very clever man that I should "work harder on myself than I do on my job." That man's name is E. James Rohn. Jim Rohn had another statement he backed himself up with: "Never wish your job were easier; wish that you were better."

It hit me like a bolt of lightning! If I stopped wishing everything was handed to me on a silver platter, wishing that everything was easy, I might actually realize that life becomes easier when I get better. Hence, business lives by those exact same rules: The better I get at business, the easier it becomes.

I'll put it really bluntly: If you're stagnant and you've stopped growing, then your business will be exactly the same. When you keep on learning and therefore growing, so will your business. And the better you get at the game of business, the more money you'll make.

Time: Your Most Valuable Asset

If every business owner only knew the definition of the term *opportunity cost*. If you waste every dollar you've ever made, you can still make it back again. Yet if you waste even a minute of your life, you'll never get another shot at it. Most business owners I've met spend their day doing things that really won't bring them long-term wealth or long-term business success. They run their own shops, make their own products, and all in the name of saving wage costs. Now, I'll be the first to admit that a new business needs to save every dollar possible and to keep overheads to a minimum, but at some stage you've got to decide to grow.

Put simply, you've got to *invest* rather than *spend* your time. As the owner of a business, you've got to be certain that every activity you undertake, every job you do, every minute of your working day is invested in doing something that only *you* can do. Always ask yourself this question: "What will give me the best *Return on Investment* (ROI) for my time?"

And remember, if it pays you back immediately with a few dollars an hour, then your business is probably losing money. I'd rather it paid me back with a few cents a day for the rest of my life. Work with the long-term in mind, not just the instant rewards.

I Know

Anyone with teenage kids knows one thing about teenagers—they *know* everything. Just ask them. Then, when you get a little older you realize that it's probably not polite to say, "I know" out loud to everyone. So as an adult we listen politely, all the while in the back of our mind saying, "I know." You probably even cross your arms.

Forget that mind-set: It's what you learn when you *think* you know everything that counts.

Intelligence is the ability to draw even finer and finer distinctions on a certain subject. Remember how that movie you saw more than once, or that book you read several times, was different the second time around? One of the fastest ways to make sure you never learn anything new, never grow, and never create more income for yourself is to continually state that you know everything. Open up your mind; it's not the major realizations that'll make you a fortune. It's the fine distinctions that give you the edge over the rest of the population.

The difference between ordinary and extraordinary is that little bit extra.

What's in a Lamb Roast?

One night at dinner, a young man asked his wife, "Why do you cut the ends off the lamb roast?" Her reply, "I'm not sure. My mother used to do it."

A week went by and they visited her mother for dinner, and you guessed it, lamb roast for dinner. So he asked, "Why do you cut the ends off the lamb roast?" Her reply: "I'm not sure. My mother always did it." So he made a phone call to his wife's grandmother and asked, "Why do you cut the ends off the lamb roast?" Her reply; "Well, I've only got a small baking tray."

So, often we do things just because it's the way we've always done them, having absolutely no idea why it was done that way to start with.

When other people *zig*, you've got to *zag*. Following the crowd will almost certainly lead you to slaughter. But you'll also notice it's rare for eagles to flock together.

In an increasingly competitive environment, you must distinguish yourself by more than just price. You do this by being different. Think about what makes you unique and then tell the world.

Taking a Look in the Mirror

I still remember the words as plain as day: "You only ever get the staff you deserve." It was on that day when my dad helped me realize everything that goes on in my business is a reflection of either my ability or my inability.

It still amazes me to this day how a business is a reflection of its owner. Some owners want to control everything and wonder why none of their team members ever take any initiative. Some hate selling and love paperwork, so they've always got their numbers done, but never really sell too much, and so on. It almost feels like your business is designed to teach you everything you don't know.

And, as my dad pointed out, the people you attract in your life are another great mirror of where you are at. It wasn't until I became a great person, a great businessman, and a great leader, that I started to attract great people.

And *attract* great people I did. When you reach this level, it's rarely necessary to go looking for people; they usually come to you.

Business Is a Self-Fulfilling Prophecy

Remember back to the last time you bought a car. All of a sudden you noticed there were hundreds of them on the road. Or here's another example: Try right now to *not* picture a pink elephant with wings in your mind. Your brain has an amazing power to create or find whatever you focus on. It's called your Reticular Activating System (RAS), and it's like your personal compass.

Your RAS will find proof that the earth is flat if you want it to. In fact, it'll find proof that November is a slow month if you want it to. In other words, attention determines direction. Just like the last time you said to yourself, "Don't forget, don't forget, don't forget." And, what happened? You forgot. Change your wording to "remember."

And here's another example: If you were to ask people how their day's been, and they answered, "Not bad," what would be their benchmark on life? *Bad*, and today's not that. Your brain is an amazing tool and it'll find whatever you ask it to find, so you'd better ask for very positive things.

Remember to ask for the things you want, *not* to push away what you don't want.

Every day your business meets your true expectations. In other words, if you believe you've got to work hard to make money, then that will always be your reality. If you believe you can never get good people, then that'll be your reality.

Remember, you generally make true whatever you believe to be so.

Taps on the Shoulder

Traveling down the road of life, it's easy to be distracted, to get off track, and to lose sight of the big picture. What's the old saying? "Can't see the forest for the trees." However, every day you're getting little taps on the shoulder: an idea that you should change what you're doing, a suggestion from someone, a hint. You either learn to take the taps, or eventually they become signposts you run into.

And the signposts are a whole lot bigger and they hurt a whole lot more. Then if you're still too blind, too stubborn, or just too stupid to read the signs, you'll stray into the path of oncoming traffic and get run over by the proverbial Mack truck.

Why do you think that most successful people are great networkers? It's because they've perfected the craft of surrounding themselves with other people and then listening—*really* listening—to what they have to say. They can in one night absorb more "taps on the shoulder" than many take on board in a whole year.

Just remember to get the facts, listen for the taps, and look for the signs. Sticking your head in the sand never helped anyone.

Building a Business versus Buying a Job

Why would you want to go into business for yourself? Just look at the statistics. Around 80 percent of businesses started this year will be gone in five years.

Most business owners seem to work harder than any of their people, and many seem to make less income than they could make elsewhere.

From what I've found, people start their own businesses for one thing and one thing only: *freedom*. Whether that is working for themselves, having more time to themselves, financial freedom, or just the freedom of knowing that they're in charge of their lives.

Many people with little interest in ever "captaining their own ship" argue that they're far from "in charge" when exposed to the volatility of owning a business. I retort with this analogy: I may have 100 different customers. You on the other hand have only one—your boss. If I lose half my customers I still have 50 left. You just need to lose one to be singing for your supper!

Yet despite this longing to be in charge, for most business owners the exact opposite becomes reality. Most end up having the businesses run them, instead of their running the businesses. In fact, they end up with the very thing they didn't want, a *job*.

In effect, they've taken great risks and expended vast energy, and all they've done is bought employment.

My Definition of a Business

Getting rid of the *job* is why you've got to understand the real definition of a business, my definition. A business is a commercial, profitable enterprise that works without *you*.

One more time: A business is a commercial, profitable enterprise that works without *you*.

Let that sink in for a moment.

I know it seems to be 180 degrees away from what you've been taught in the past. Think about it: why build a job for yourself, when you can build an income stream that keeps on growing whether you're there or not? Remember this one simple fact: The only reason you would ever start a business is to sell it. Your business is your product, it's what you're building, and it's where you're ultimately going to make your profit—selling the business.

Very few people ever make a fortune running their businesses, but a lot of people make a fortune selling them.

Look at Bill Gates, for instance. Sure he's made a lot of money selling software, but he became the richest man in the world by selling shares in his business, Microsoft.

Are you too involved in your business? Could you pick up the phone in the morning and say to whoever answered, "You guys look after things. I'm taking three months off?" If you're like the vast majority of business owners out there, the answer would definitely be *no*.

On Not *In*

It's for this very reason that you have to get yourself out of the day-to-day routine of the business. Stop working 9:00 till 5:00, doing the work of your business. It's like the carpenters that don't run their businesses. Instead, they spend all day using a hammer and nails, working *in* their business.

Imagine that when you started your business, you built it in your mind first, and then you drew a picture on paper of what it would be like when it was finished. That's right. You've got to finish a business at some stage and have it ready for sale.

As an example, imagine buying this book after I'd slapped together only an outline of each chapter, before I finished writing it. How much would you pay for it? Only a fraction of its full price. The same happens in business. People try to sell a business that hasn't been finished, so they're really only selling a *job*. Of course, they'd only ever get a fraction of the price for it.

When you've got the finished picture, then you go to work creating that business. That means working *on* the business, rather than just *in* the business.

In fact, you're designing the business so it will run whether you're there or not. Then you've got choice, and choice to me equates to freedom. You can keep the business, or you can sell it. You can work in the business, or you can spend your time more creatively.

You Work Hard Because Your Business Doesn't

Now imagine a business like that for a moment, where you didn't have to work there. Would the business *work*? I mean would it function properly? Would all of the systems and the people integrate to get the result you wanted, the result your customer wanted? *Of course it would.*

Almost all business owners I've ever met work so hard *(too hard)* for this exact reason. Their businesses don't work; they do. Everything about the businesses is in their heads, and they're the only ones who can do anything, so they're trapped. Imagine my example of this book and how hard I'd have to work if this knowledge were only in my head.

Most owners are like this because they don't trust anyone else to do the job. For some reason they believe that no one can do it as well as they can. They have to be in control.

Take the step, start to document how everything in your business gets done, put systems in place, teach other people, and give them the responsibility to get the job done. (Read Michael Gerber's book, *"The E-Myth,"* for more on this.)

All great leaders are good at delegating, so start off-loading some of the tasks *now*!

By the way, once you've given them the job to do, let them do it. Don't jump in and save them; that way they'll never learn how to get the job done. All they will learn is that you're the only one who can fix things, so you always will. Remember, sometimes you have to let them fall off the bike to learn how to stay on.

Work for Yourself and Go the Extra Mile

All that you've just read doesn't excuse you if you're working in a business that's owned by someone else. Remember, what goes around comes around, so give it everything you've got. Always go that little bit further than you're asked to, give a little extra, and you'll go far. If you're asked to stay till 5:00 p.m., stay until 5:30 p.m. Just do a little more than you're asked.

By the way, this goes for your customers as well. Don't just satisfy them. A satisfied customer never tells anyone about you. Give them something more than they expected, go the extra mile, delight them so that they send their friends your way.

One last point here: The real reason to have a job is to get paid while doing your market research. Work for people you can learn from, in a business where you can learn as much as you can about the business you want to run in the future, about business in general, or about any subject that interests you.

The Key to Success Is Laziness

Here's a controversial one but I'd rather have 1 percent of 100 peoples' income than 100 percent of my own. If you've ever thought that you'll succeed if you just work a little harder, put in some extra time, or just do more of what you're doing right now, then it's time you lifted your head and took a look around you.

Thousands of people you know all work hard, but they're not really getting anywhere.

The aim of the game isn't to work harder; it's to create better results with less effort—finding ways of achieving more with less. In other words, to continually leverage your time, your efforts, your money, and your knowledge.

If you're paid an hourly wage, you'll never earn more than the number of hours you work, but if you and your business are set up so that you're paid whether you work or not, then you've truly understood one of the key principles of success: *Leverage* to have more. Play my board game *"Leverage,"* the fun way to learn about business.

Leverage is simply the ability to do more with less. You see, employees earn money and business owners make money. Now take that one step further: Entrepreneurs and investors collect money.

The aim of the game is to create an income stream that flows whether you work or not. Build assets that yield income.

Change: Agrarian, Industrial, Information Age

For many years now people have misunderstood how money is made. People still seem to think farming is a way to riches. Well, consider this. At the turn of the twentieth century, around 95 percent of the population worked the land. The wealthiest people were the landowners.

Come the 1950s, 1960s, 1970s and even into the early 1980s, people who made things made the majority of money. The Japanese economy boomed, as they could make it cheaper, faster, and better than anyone else.

Americans cried foul, as they thought Japanese VCRs would kill their economy. Now, the Americans have learned their lesson: It's not the VCRs that make all the money; it's making a movie that plays on the VCRs that does.

In the information age we're living through, it only takes about 18 months for the available information on the planet to double. Just think about that. A century ago it took about 50 years to double our knowledge. And, if you're looking closely, it's the people who have and sell the information who now make all the money.

Can't Be Cheaper, Can't Have a Better Product, and Don't Need a Better Product

With information moving so fast, people can copy, reproduce, and have ready for sale any product or service in a matter of weeks.

In today's world, you can't be cheaper than your competitors for long. You can't be far better than anyone else for long, so you've got to know that information is the key to business success.

The only way you can stay ahead of the market is to outthink, outsell, outmarket, and outmaneuver your competitors. Marketing is crucial. You don't have to have the world's best hamburger to sell billions of them.

The next time you have a group of people in a room, ask them who thinks McDonald's has the best hamburgers in the world. I'll bet very few people will put their hands up. Yet who sells more hamburgers than anyone else?

Then ask the same group if they could build a better sales, marketing, and distribution system for hamburgers than McDonald's. Once again I bet no one will put up their hands.

It all comes down to systems and marketing.

Sell Pans

In fact, if you want to sell billions of something, all you've got to do is find a gold rush and stand on the side of the road selling pans. Everyone needs a pan.

So many people rush in and start digging for gold, and yet the people who make the most money don't have to work hard all day digging for customers; they just need to find a massive flow of customers and help them to buy.

Don't go against a trend; don't try to sell to people who don't want to buy. Just stand by the road and sell to people who desperately want to buy. You only need one thing to make a fortune in the restaurant business: *a starving crowd.*

Think of the 12-year-old who stands on the street corner cleaning car windows. The market already exists; the 12-year-old just fills a need.

If you've got a product or a service that everyone wants, then it'll sell itself. Marketing is so simple when you stand in the path of people who really want to buy rather than your having to go out there to sell.

Ask for More

If you're going to build a great business, if you're going to make your fortune through business, then you've got to ask for a whole lot more than you do right now.

My mom used to always tell me that I should never get my hopes up in case it didn't come together. As much as I love my mom, in my opinion, the opposite is true. Shoot for the stars; at least you'll make it to the moon.

If you don't ask, the answer is always *no*. If you start to ask for more and are grateful for it, you just might start receiving. Just remember, those who are grateful always receive more than those who just complain about life.

And don't be afraid of someone saying *no*. They are not rejecting you. It's just that your request may have come at a bad time, or that their goals aren't quite aligned with yours. Don't take offense. Every *no* gets you closer to a *yes*.

I've always said that you'll only ever be as big as your competition. If your competition is putting food on the table, that's how big you can get. If your competition is making a million dollars profit this year, that's how big you can get. At *Action International*, our competition is stated in our vision. *World Abundance through Business Re-education*. In other words, our competition is world abundance, it's enormous, and that's how big we can get.

Abundance versus Scarcity

And while you're asking for more, you'd better understand that for most people getting more means that someone else has to go without. Nothing could be further from the truth.

There is literally more than enough to go around. Scarcity was first espoused by the English preacher Thomas Malthus, who worked out that England would run out of food, as there were too many people for food production, yet even to this day we still produce more than enough food to feed the entire planet. Yet because we believe in scarcity *(this is more commonly known as supply and demand)*, much of it gets thrown away.

In business, you've got to realize that there is always more than enough money to go around. The question is, when will you go out and get your share?

Abundance is a mind-set, a mind-set that understands how technology has removed scarcity. How the old thoughts in economics are exactly that—old.

How Much Do You Earn?

Just to prove that thinking differently is so important, write down how much money you earned last year. Now add a zero to the end of it. You've just increased your income tenfold.

If you were to make that much money doing exactly what you're doing right now, how hard would you have to work?

You've got to stop working harder, and start working smarter. And by the way, notice this one thing about money. Remember, people with jobs *earn* money, people in their own business *make* money, and entrepreneurs *create* money.

Summing Up

Far too many people think that what you *do* is the major determinant to your success. Yet for me, it's always been a very simple formula for success. *Be,* then *do,* then *have.*

Everything you've just read is about who I am. In other words, my *being.* This next chapter is about my *be.* Then we're going to get into the *do,* so you can *have* whatever it is you want to have.

Be the person you need to *be,* in order to *do* the things you need to *do,* in order to *have* the things you want to *have.*

Part 2

■ How to Become a Marketing Genius

This chapter concerns your mental approach. Its main aim is to get you to think about marketing in a whole different way. It's about smashing the traditional approach that stipulates that marketing be considered an expense. As you'll see, it is not.

It's time to unlock the amazingly simple truth about marketing, an area of business that so often eludes comprehension, yet it's by far the most important ingredient of being a success.

Cost Reduction versus Income Growth

So many businesspeople focus their whole lives on cost reduction, working long hours just to save a wage, cutting costs just to make ends meet. Now don't get me wrong, keeping your costs down is still one of the most important areas of business, but...

If you really want to make money, you've got to put more of your time into income generation than you do cost cutting. Just a few hours a day focused on income generation can pay for the wages of several people.

Making 10 times, or even 100 times more profit than you do right now is more about increasing your income than it is about decreasing your costs.

By the way, if you were to cut your costs by as much as you possibly could and still leave your company running, you'd probably only add about 10 or 20 percent to your bottom line. Yet through building your income, the bottom-line jump is limitless.

Distribution and Marketing

It's important noting that business has two major parts. And both of them are equally as important as the other.

You've got to put 50 percent of your time, effort, and investment into distribution—getting your products and services to the marketplace. The other half of your time should be spent on sales and marketing—getting the marketplace to come to your products and services.

The challenge is that most business owners, and therefore their entire businesses, put about 90 percent of their time into distribution and only about 10 percent into marketing. You've got to market if you're ever going to make real money.

Focus on Cashflow

Just to stress this point even more—if you're not focused on creating cashflow, then you're wasting your time in business.

Anyone can create a business that's no more than just a job and make a living from it, but very few will ever create a massive cashflow goldmine. If that's what you're after, then you've got to understand that profit is the difference between cashflow in and cashflow out. Neither is more important than the other, but the in flow is where you get exponential growth.

Marketing: Expense or Investment?

Most accountants will show you that sales, marketing, and advertising fall into the expense side of your business, and I know when you're signing the checks it can certainly feel that way. Yet, when it's done properly, marketing is your best investment.

Think about it this way. If you were to run a $1000 advertisement that returned you $2000 in profit in a matter of weeks, then you'd be doubling your money. And what's more, you can run that ad as many times as you like because it never costs you anything; it always makes you money. Sounds like a great investment to me. Marketing is only an expense when done incorrectly.

What most businesspeople don't understand is how to take the marketing and advertising they're doing right now from the expense column and move it across to become an investment.

Test and Measure

So, this is the answer. The only way to become a marketing genius is to simply test and measure. Ask every customer who walks through the door, every caller, every prospect you ever deal with, this one simple question: "By the way, how did you find out about us?"

And simply keep a tally.

Remember, you cannot manage what you cannot measure. This way you'll very quickly find out what marketing works, what pays for itself, and what is just an expense. Of course, you'll either change the ads that are an expense, or stop running them all together.

Then, for exponential growth all you have to do is refocus every dollar you spent on what didn't work, to those that do, and then every dollar you spend on marketing will make you dollar after dollar.

Yet despite this logic, it's amazing how many business owners still blindly spend their marketing budget without measuring the results. What's the use of placing a $250 ad in the local paper, if you're lucky to get $150 worth of business from it? Of course there isn't any.

Problem is, many people think the ad is bringing in much more business than it really is because they don't properly test and measure.

Compare it to sports. When was the last time you watched a football game or tennis match and nobody kept score? It's the same for business. You've got to keep score of everything you do. After all, if you don't know you've got a problem, how can you fix it?

Another challenge here is that your accountant will teach you to measure the wrong things. As an accountant, I can firmly tell you that measuring turnover, costs, and profit is a waste of time. In Part 3, we'll look at the things you need to measure.

Acquisition Cost

Imagine having to work out how much your business should spend on sales and marketing. Setting a budget is as hard as finding a needle in a haystack.

Let me show you how you can have an unlimited marketing budget, and buy—that's right, *buy*—as many customers as you want. It's like turning on the tap to business profits.

Instead of spending a fixed amount, when you take on the idea of investing in sales and marketing you've got to understand that every investment has a purchase price. In business most people think that you just invest in the stock you sell, but the same is true of customers.

In fact, from a marketing point of view, the only thing you've got to buy are new customers. The question is, how much are you paying for them?

If you've put $1000 into advertising and had 100 phone calls, then you're paying $10 for a lead. Then if you only sell to 1 in 5 of those leads, you're paying $50 (5 × $10) for a sale.

Now, here's where this all gets exciting.

Imagine that you knew you could create a marketing plan that buys a customer for $50 and on average they'd spend $500 with you, of which $100 was profit. Then how many times could you invest that $50?

As many times as you want. Spend $50, make $100.

Sounds too good to be true, doesn't it? But it really is that simple! Once you know how much it costs to buy a customer, and as long as you make more per customer than the acquisition cost, you're ready to start reaping the profits.

Buying a Customer

The difference is huge. When you switch from selling to new customers to focusing on buying new ones, you'll start to see a whole new, unlimited world of sales and marketing results.

Try to see the entire function of your business as nothing more than a buying exercise. An exercise of buying customers, *not* selling products or services. Then the only real question you've got to ask is, can you buy customers for less than they'll spend over their lifetimes of buying?

As soon as you start to see your business as a total marketing entity, *not* a production, service, or retail entity, you'll understand why the price you pay for customers is your biggest expense.

Here is something even more powerful. What if you could buy them for less than your profits on your first sale, and what if that first sale came within days of the commencement of your marketing campaign?

It's around this time in the learning cycle that people start getting really excited. And it's only the beginning, because when we start getting customers to keep coming back and spending more per visit, that's when real wealth starts accumulating.

Wallet Share versus Market Share

Chasing market share in today's business world is a guaranteed formula for chasing your tail. If buying customers is your biggest expense, then continually buying new customers *(buying market share)* is the most expensive way to do business.

Market share, or a focus on new customers, comes with an assumption that you're in the business of buying products or services and selling them to customers. If, however, you move to the idea of buying customers, then your whole ballpark changes. You're no longer chasing market share, you're chasing wallet share. The issue becomes how much, how many, and for how long can you sell to each customer you buy.

In this world of business, where customer loyalty is everything, you've got to know that if you've already spent the money to buy a customer, then it makes total sense to make sure you get a full return on that customer *(your investment)*.

Chasing wallet share is as simple as remembering that you've got a loyal customer base, so what else can you sell to your customers?

What Business Are You In?

Most businesspeople define their business by what they sell, like a fruit shop, an accounting service, and so on.

Change from a product or service point of view to a marketing point of view and you'll realize you're now in the *profit*-making business. And making a profit is as simple as spending less than you earn. In other words, you've got to buy customers, with your sales and marketing, for less than they spend with you, either by cutting the cost of buying a customer, or by extending the amount people will spend with you over their lifetimes of buying.

It's fairly basic mathematics but it isn't taught in too many business schools.

Lifetime Value

Think about this for a moment. How much are you going to spend in your lifetime on something as simple as toilet paper? Thousands of dollars?

So let me ask you this. How much will average customers in your business spend with you over their lifetimes?

Let me give you an example. In my dog food business, average people will spend $800 a year on their dogs, and the average dog lives for 10 years. So, assuming a customer stays with me for only half of that time, 5 years, then she is worth $4000 to me.

Then, what if my customers all refer to me two new customers in their first year. Now they're worth three times $4000: This equals $12,000.

What if they also then referred another two every year, and every referral sent us another two customers a year. How much are they worth to me now? Hundreds of thousands? Or, more to the point, how much are your customers worth to you over their lifetimes of buying from you?

You must establish this long-term view of their value before you can appreciate how important it is to develop a relationship with customers and to ensure that everything is done to keep them for as long as possible.

A Promotion versus a Business

That brings up an amazingly powerful business point. What's the difference between a business and a promotion?

Many businesspeople have just a promotion and go through life thinking it's a business. Let me explain. In a promotion, you have one product, one service, and once you've sold it to someone, that's it. You've got to go out and find yourself another customer. That's an ongoing marketing promotion, *not* a business.

On the other hand, a business is where you buy customers and then sell something, or many things, to them over and over and over again. By the way, whoever said you can't sell someone else's products or services and get paid a commission for the referral?

Strategic alliances with other businesses can be a very powerful way to increase your customer base for a relatively low outlay. And, what's more, by linking up with the right businesses, you can target the exact type of customer who offers the best return on your acquisition cost.

In Summary

After reading this chapter, you should experience a profound mind-set change towards marketing. I hope this has already taken place.

From now on if you think of marketing strictly as an investment, of customers as something you *buy*, then you will start spending at least 50 percent of your time in this area of the business. If this hasn't already happened, read the chapter again!

I've seen these simple instructions completely transform thousands of businesses who have been stuck on the treadmill of traditional thinking.

It's time to get off the treadmill and start getting somewhere.

Once you've accepted these philosophies and are prepared to make the necessary changes to your business, that's when you can start applying the tips included in the last part. The first three parts will get you ready. The fourth will give you all the tips and the tools to make it happen.

But before anything can happen, you need to meet my mechanic.

Part 3

∎ My Mechanic and the Business Chassis

It hadn't been a good day for Charlie, my mechanic. Given that I love cars but know very little about the technical workings of them, Charlie and I had gotten to know each other quite well.

Our conversations had always been pretty one dimensional—about cars and Italian cooking—until today, when I was greeted by an obviously frustrated businessman—a small businessman desperate to get bigger.

"What's paining you, Charlie?" I asked while slowly backing my car in for new tires and a wheel alignment.

"You don't want to know," he answered softly while taking a painful sip of his badly brewed coffee.

"OK, fine. I'll take a seat in the waiting room while you install the tires. Oh, and Charlie."

"Yes, Brad,"

"Can you check the brake pads while you're at it? I spent all yesterday at the race track."

"Sure, no problem."

I was about halfway through reading a magazine article chronicling the tragedies of the Monaco royal family, when Charlie popped his head around the corner.

"Brad, I've got to ask you something. Something I've been wanting to ask for some time."

"Go ahead, shoot."

"You drive these incredible sports cars that I love working on, you never seem stressed or rushed, you're always taking trips away and doing things just for fun. And money, you never seem to be short there either. How the heck do you manage it?"

Before I could offer any opinion, Charlie caught his breath.

"Here I am, a damn good mechanic, I work my backside off six, sometimes seven days a week, and yet I barely make enough to have any leftover for fun. And even if I did, when would I have the time to enjoy it?"

I didn't think the dramatic monologue was over. He didn't let me down.

"I think I'm doing all I can. Each month I place ads in the local paper, I do mailbox drops, and occasionally I even do spots on radio.

"It seems like things pick up when we do a spurt of advertising, but it's often followed by a trough, and at the end of the month it can be a battle to cover the overheads."

Charlie wasn't the first person I'd met with this affliction, a person working for himself, but really just owning a job.

It quickly became clear that just like our conversations had been one-dimensional in the past, so too had Charlie's perception of how to make a business more profitable. His mantra was simple: Throw a few ads here and there and then let's hope enough people pick up the phone or walk through the door to make it all worthwhile.

He was certainly telling the truth about his craftsmanship. Charlie is a first-rate mechanic. I always feel totally comfortable entrusting my repairs to him.

As for the business, well to me, it seemed to have great potential. More than just your average garage, he also had a small spare parts division and a detailing service. All together he had four people working for him.

I waited to see if he was finished. He opened his mouth, but it was just to accommodate a big sigh.

"Charlie, my friend, you'll probably be surprised to know that my entire professional philosophy is based on what I call the Business Chassis."

I caught his glare of bewilderment.

"You know, like the chassis of a car."

His expression didn't change.

"Let me explain. Just like the old VW chassis that were used to build the initial Porsche cars, you too can transform your business. You can stick with one that'll keep going forever, making a few dollars here and there, or you can build an amazingly powerful, superproducing, profit-yielding business. The choice is yours."

Charlie's eyes were boring into mine.

"What you're about to learn is guaranteed to be the most powerful business secret you'll ever learn, as long as you make sure you're using it every day."

Charlie's expression had now gone from bewilderment to deep skepticism.

Undeterred, I started explaining to Charlie, as I'd done hundreds of times before, the Business Chassis.

The Business Chassis

Most people don't really understand business and, therefore, work too hard. In fact, most businesspeople work on the three areas of the chassis that refer to results, instead of the areas that can transform the business into a profit powerhouse. You'll see what I mean in a minute. First, let me explain the parts of the chassis.

Your Number of Leads

1) **Leads:** The total number of potential buyers that you contacted or that contacted you last year. Also known as prospects, or potentials. Most business-people confuse responses, or the number of potential buyers, with results. Just because the phone is ringing doesn't mean the cash register is. And, what's even

more amazing is that very few businesses even know how many leads they get a week, let alone from each and every marketing campaign. It's great to get a lot of leads, but then you've got to remember your...

Conversion Rate

2) **Conversion Rate:** The percentage of people who did buy as opposed to those who could have bought. For example, if you had 10 people walk through your store today and you sold to only 3 of them, you'd have a conversion rate of 3 out of 10, or 30 percent. This has got to be a literal gold mine in almost every business I walk into. You've already got them interested; now you've just got to get them over the line. When I ask average business owners about their conversion rate, they take a stab in the dark and tell me that it's between 60 and 70 percent. Just for fun, I get them to measure it, and a couple of weeks later we find that it's more like 20 or 30 percent. Imagine how you'd feel.

You should feel great, in fact you should be excited, because if you're getting by at 20 or 30 percent, imagine how your business would run at 60 or 70 percent. Remember, double your conversion rate and you've just doubled your turnover.

Your Number of Customers

Number of Customers: This is the number of different customers you deal with. You work it out by multiplying the total number of leads by the conversion rate. I'll run through an example in just a moment. Remember, *it's not about getting more customers.* You can't change that number. It's about getting more leads and then improving your conversion rate. These are the variables that lead to the result.

Your Number of Transactions

3) **Number of Transactions:** Another of the five main variables. Some of your customers will buy from you weekly, others monthly, others on the odd occasion, and others just once in a lifetime. What you want to know now is the average. Not your best and not your worst, but the average number of times one of your customers buys from you in a year. Once again, here's another gold mine; most businesspeople never collect a database of their past customers, let alone write to them, or call them and ask them to come back.

Your Average Dollar Sale

4) Average Dollar Sale: Here's one variable that at least some business owners do measure. Once again, some might spend $5000, some just $5, but the average is what you're after. Just a few dollars on each and every sale could be all it takes to calculate. Add up your total sales and divide it by the number of sales.

Your Turnover

Your Turnover: Another result. Multiply the total number of customers you dealt with by the number of times they came back on average, and then by the average amount they spent with you each time. That's your turnover. Put simply, Customers x Transactions x Average $ Sale = Turnover. This is another area most business owners will know the answer to. Yet they most probably have no real idea how they got to it. Of course, you want more of it, but *you can't get more turnover.* What you can get is more transactions and a higher average dollar sale with the total number of customers you deal with.

Your Margins

5) Margins: This is the percentage of each and every sale that's profit. In other words, if you sold something for $100 and $25 was profit, then you've got a 25 percent margin. Remember: This is after all costs are taken out. It's potentially another little gold mine for you to tap into.

Your Profits

Profit: Another result that every business owner wants more of, not realizing that *you can't get more profit,* but what you can get is greater margins on the turnover you've got.

And that's it.

The Business Chassis I outlined to Charlie is the basic model that dictates the profit levels of every business on earth.

By simply breaking down your business and marketing efforts *(selling is married to marketing)* into these five areas and understanding how each affects the other, you're halfway there—and way ahead of 90 percent of businesses out there.

Now, Let's Try it with a Few Numbers

To bring all of this home to you, let's put in some numbers that should help you make sense of it all.

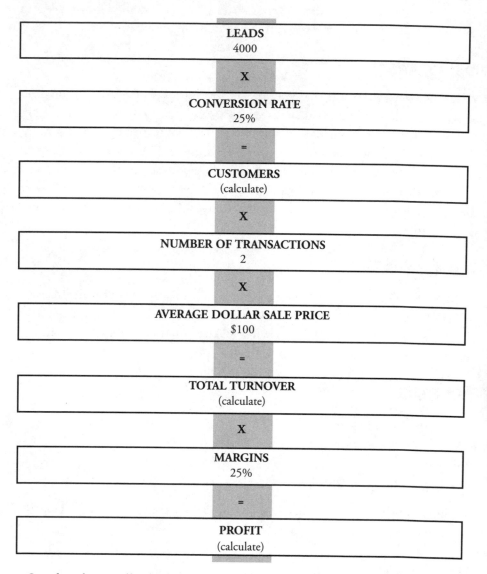

LEADS
4000

X

CONVERSION RATE
25%

=

CUSTOMERS
(calculate)

X

NUMBER OF TRANSACTIONS
2

X

AVERAGE DOLLAR SALE PRICE
$100

=

TOTAL TURNOVER
(calculate)

X

MARGINS
25%

=

PROFIT
(calculate)

So what does it all calculate out to?

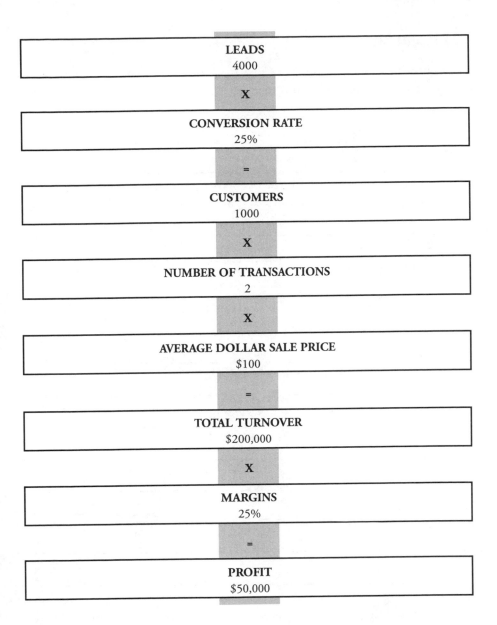

Now, I'll show you the power of this simple little chassis.

A 10 Percent Rise

All you do is increase each and every area that's highlighted by just 10 percent. You might want to grab a calculator to check my workings.

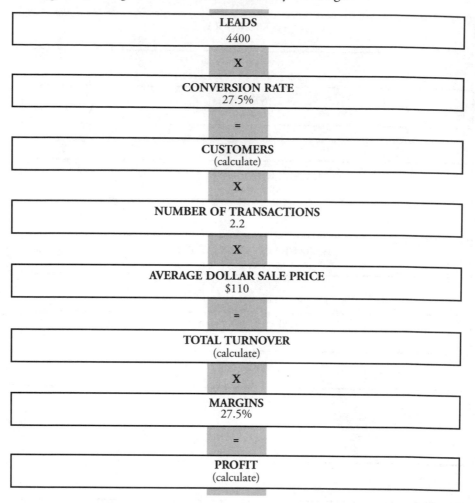

| LEADS |
| 4400 |

X

| CONVERSION RATE |
| 27.5% |

=

| CUSTOMERS |
| (calculate) |

X

| NUMBER OF TRANSACTIONS |
| 2.2 |

X

| AVERAGE DOLLAR SALE PRICE |
| $110 |

=

| TOTAL TURNOVER |
| (calculate) |

X

| MARGINS |
| 27.5% |

=

| PROFIT |
| (calculate) |

So, of course, what you've done is increase your turnover and profits by 10 percent, haven't you? Well, haven't you?

Or, has something extra happened?

Get ready for a pleasant surprise!

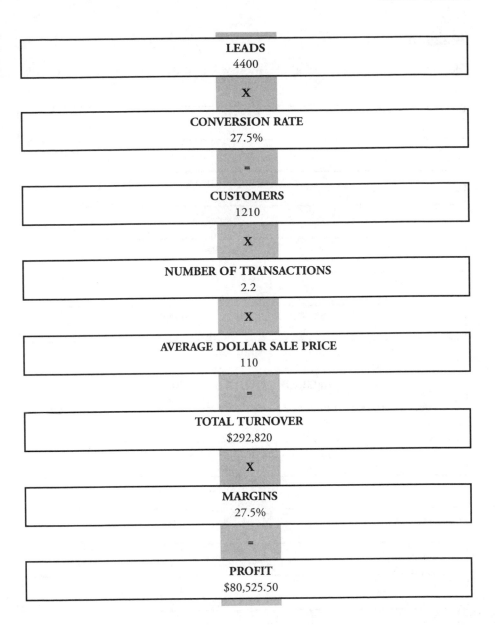

Yes, it actually works. Just by adding 10 percent in each and every area, you'll add a massive 61 percent to your take home profits. Exciting stuff, huh!

Now, just for a little fun, let's do this exercise:

Double Up

Let's imagine that over a period of time you could double each of the five areas:

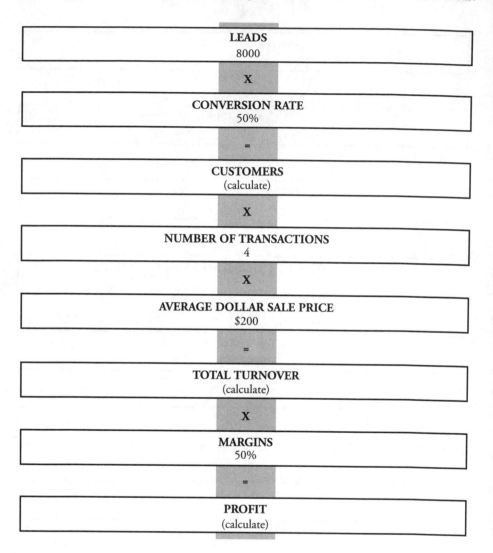

LEADS
8000

X

CONVERSION RATE
50%

=

CUSTOMERS
(calculate)

X

NUMBER OF TRANSACTIONS
4

X

AVERAGE DOLLAR SALE PRICE
$200

=

TOTAL TURNOVER
(calculate)

X

MARGINS
50%

=

PROFIT
(calculate)

So, what's it add, or should I say, multiply out to? Think you've just doubled your profits? Wrong—dead wrong!

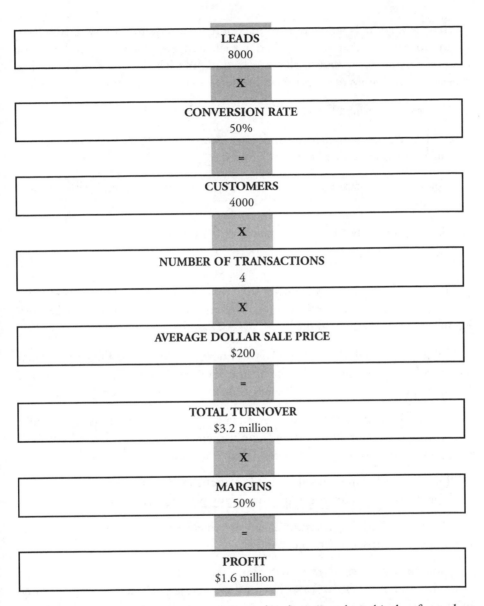

I know it seems almost outrageous to be throwing these kinds of numbers around, but it really works. I mean calculators don't lie!

"Remember the word *Kaizen*, Charlie," I said, as my explanation was coming to an end.

"It's the way the Japanese refer to the ability to always improve your results. It means to get just that little bit better each and every day. It literally means *constant improvement*. And, if all you can do is add just 1% per week in each of these five areas, or even 1% per month, then you can work out the possibilities."

"*Kaizen*," confirmed Charlie. "I'll remember that."

But I could see that Charlie was far from convinced. It seemed such a shame. So much potential, yet so little of it realized.

"You don't seem ready to take on the world, my friend," I said with a hint of frustration.

"Sure I'm ready, but it's much easier said than done, Brad."

Oh, if only I had a dollar...

"I follow all that stuff you said about the chassis, but how am I actually going to make those improvements? It seems to work, but how can I make it happen? I don't see what more I can do."

"I'll make you a deal, Charlie. Over the next couple of days I'll get you to tag along with me as I visit some of the businesses the Coaching Team at *Action* and I have helped to turn around. All you've got to do is watch, listen, and emulate."

"The tricks of the trade are pretty much the same for any industry, so you've just got to take their strategies and apply them to your business. It's all fairly straightforward and remarkably simple, but it all comes back to you."

"First you've got to be open-minded so that the ideas are absorbed, and then you've got to be disciplined enough to actually put these strategies into practice."

"But won't these businesspeople get all secretive and defensive when I start looking over their shoulder?" he asked.

"Not for a second," I reassured him. "They all know there's plenty to go around. And it's not like we're spying on them. We're just watching my teachings in practice. Teachings I'm as happy to share as they are."

He pondered this by rubbing the back of his stubby neck.

"Besides, that's the least of their concerns. If people come knocking it's because they've implemented my suggestions, and as a result their business is booming.

Apart from being enormously rewarding, it offers great networking opportunities."

I could tell he was interested.

"Hopefully people will come knocking on your door in the near future."

I could see he was starting to warm to the whole idea.

"Do we have a deal?" I asked, hand extended.

"But who will run my business? The next couple of days are fully booked."

"In light of what I've just offered, that seems a trivial problem indeed. In fact, it will be the first lesson: learn to delegate. If you can pass that, we will move on to the first grade."

With a small degree of angst he slowly shook my hand.

"That's it, then, 9:00 a.m. sharp I'll come around and pick you up."

"Okay."

An hour later my car was finished and as usual Charlie had performed faultlessly. This is the start of a rewarding few days, I thought to myself.

Charlie Meets Barry, the Cake Shop Owner, for a Lesson on Boosting Leads

The bloodshot eyes told me Charlie hadn't slept very much last night. It was quite clear he'd been up most of the early hours either talking to his wife or just staring at the ceiling, deep in thought.

That was a good sign.

"Good morning, my pupil," I said teasingly.

"Hello, Brad," replied Charlie, obviously not in the mood for humorous repartee.

No matter, he had found someone to look after his shop and was ready for the day's excursion.

"Do you like chocolate éclairs?" I asked.

"I guess. Haven't had one in years though."

As we headed towards Barry's cake shop, I tried to impress on Charlie the importance of having an open mind, of seeing the need for change, and of being brave enough to try something new. I don't know why, but it's often the least happy business owners that are the most reluctant to change.

"Welcome to our first classroom, Charlie," I chirped as we were greeted by Barry.

I had spoken to Barry the night before and he was ready with a big smile when we arrived. I could see Charlie starting to breathe a little easier.

Barry had sought my advice in a similar way to what Charlie had. I had been a regular customer and he'd gotten to know what I did with my company *Action International*. One day we started talking about things other than pastries, and it became blatantly apparent that he was caught in the same trap most get tangled in.

"Brad, the only advertising I do really is a weekly ad in the local paper. I think it helps out but I'd certainly like more customers," he offered lamely the first time we discussed his lead generation strategies.

I relayed this to Charlie who was mesmerized by the variety and volume of different cakes, pastries, breads, and cookies on display.

The first thing we did with Barry was to immediately begin testing and measuring the effectiveness of his marketing. I specifically wanted to know how much each new customer *cost* him.

This project took a week as Barry asked every new person who came into the bakery where they heard about him from. To Barry's shock the ad, which was costing $300 a week, attracted only 30 new customers each week. And since each customer was only spending an average of $4.50, it was actually costing more to attract customers than they were spending in the shop.

His *acquisition cost* per new customer from the ad was $10.00—more than the average spent and thus totally unacceptable.

The key lesson I wanted Charlie to learn from Barry's experience was the importance of testing and measuring. "You see how important it is to track every piece of marketing you do," I said.

Once we started testing and measuring, Barry's approach to marketing changed forever. He started to focus on results-driven campaigns with a low acquisition cost. There would be no more blind forays with money thrown about in the hope some of it would work.

Instead of the usual "Call in to Barry's Bakery for a great choice of the freshest breads" type of ad that you see everywhere, we decided to try something a little different.

I asked Barry, "How much do your chocolate éclairs sell for?"

"$2.50," he replied.

"OK, how much do they cost you to make?"

With a tinge of embarrassment he replied, "30 cents."

"Great. That means we have a product offering great perceived value that really costs you very little. Let's start giving them away."

After a little convincing we spent the same $300 in the local paper, but this time the headline simply read, "Free Chocolate Eclair."

The response was enormous, and it was a cinch to test and measure. At the end of the week we counted 229 coupons.

All up the campaign had cost Barry $68.70 in éclairs and $300 for the ad— $368.70 in total. Now do you think all those 229 people simply came into the bakery to collect their éclairs? Of course not. Sure some did, but by Barry's calculations the average spent from the coupon crowd was $6.50—you try going into a bakery shop and stopping with one éclair.

Let's look at the new acquisition cost. It was now costing Barry only $1.61 per new customer *(this includes the cost of the éclairs)*. That means these new customers, on average, were outspending their acquisition cost by $4.89.

This basic little change, which started with testing and measuring, focusing on the customer's *acquisition cost* as well as getting a little creative, completely changed the marketing strategies of Barry's Bakery.

We also decided to take the back page of the local school newsletter that goes to all parents with a similar offer. That cost only $100 and the results were astonishing.

"And the best part, Charlie," said Barry, "is that once I get them through the door with the free éclair offer, I often get them as long-term customers. I make money right off the bat, and then it consolidates as they keep coming back."

"That's fine for a bakery, but what about a mechanic? I can't just be giving away stuff."

Barry answered for me. "Charlie, Brad and his team have more than 70 strategies to get more leads, and hundreds of ways to use each one. So you'll never be stuck. Your Coach will always help you through."

Little did Charlie know that the first new marketing strategy for his business would be a free wheel alignment, an alignment that has a perceived value of $60 or more and which would actually cost Charlie very little at all. And once the car is in the garage there are limitless opportunities of scoring more work, both on the spot and for the next time the car needs a full service.

With a bag of complimentary donuts in hand, we said good-bye to Barry and left.

Charlie and I Take a Ride and Talk about One of the Most Powerful Ways to Boost Conversion Rates

"That was the first part of the chassis, Charlie. Understanding how to get more leads, learning the importance of testing and measuring, and then remembering to focus on strategies that bring down the acquisition cost of your new customers."

"I can certainly see how it's changed Barry's business," was all Charlie offered.

"The principle is exactly the same for everyone."

Our next excursion was a trip along the highway. I wanted to expose Charlie to some billboards that advertised everything from hair care to chocolate bars.

"Charlie, now that we've looked at a simple way of getting people through your door, remember that it's only 1 of 70 or so I'm going to teach you. I want you to focus on how you make them actually pull out their wallets and make a purchase."

As we drove, I continued: "Take a look at all the advertising you see around us as we drive along and tell me what the really good ads usually have in common."

After about five minutes, he said, "I don't know Brad. They all seem quite different."

"Forget about the images and color for a minute. Focus instead on the words. What is the ad saying?"

After another five minutes, Charlie replied, "They all say they are the best in some way."

"Yes, Charlie, but look even closer. You'll find that the most successful ads actually promise that they are better. And that's what it's all about. You have to find out what your customer's number-one concern is in doing business with you and then promise them that it won't happen.

"Domino's Pizza put themselves on the map when the company promised '30 minutes or it's free.' Domino's had identified that as the key concern of people calling up for a pizza—that it wouldn't be delivered on time."

"This simple guarantee, or Unique Selling Position (USP) as the marketing folk refer to it, made Domino's a household name."

I let that sink in for a minute, then continued. "Charlie, what are you going to promise your customers?"

"I guess they want to know that I do a good job and that any part I replace won't break down again."

"Of course, they do," I responded. "When going to a mechanic, it's all about peace of mind. You're absolutely right, Charlie."

This made him feel good.

"Now, give me your business card," I demanded.

I could sense he was suddenly beginning to feel uneasy.

"Where does it say any of this on your card? Where does it say that you promise the best work in town and guarantee the quality and longevity of your repairs?"

Now Charlie was feeling bad.

"Don't get depressed about it, Charlie. The good news is that you know what your customers need reassuring about. So it's just a matter of putting that into one line and then plastering it everywhere: on your business cards, letterhead, and on all advertising and marketing material. And it should be clearly displayed for all to see in your shop as well."

I had his full attention, and pressed on a little further.

"And if you're unaware what your customers' concerns and wants really are, get them in a room and ask them. That's the best research you can do."

"Is it as simple as that?" he asked.

"You're catching on, Charlie. Now also remember that most people are born followers, so it helps conversion rates tremendously if you have plenty of great testimonials on hand. Testimonials tell people that it's OK; they're not the first to try this product. It's worked for others so it will work for them too."

"I know this can be effective, Brad, but I don't like to be pushy with my customers. I feel it's enough that they're doing business with me."

"Rubbish. If anything, it should help cement the relationship. You start by telling them what valued customers they are and how proud you'd be if they could write a few lines about your relationship.

"If you approach it the right way it has nothing but positive implications. And when you've gathered a few testimonials, pick out the best line or two and use them like the movie studios do," I continued.

"Have a look at the advertising for the latest film releases and you'd be hard-pressed to find a single one that doesn't feature positive reviews from various critics. It can work exactly the same for you."

"You've been doing business with me for a while, Brad." he stammered. "What do you say to a short testimonial when you get the chance?"

"You're catching on, Charlie. You'll have one by this time tomorrow."

His face lit up.

"One last thing," I continued as we neared our destination. "Have you ever had sales training, or do you use sales scripts in your business?"

Once again Charlie looked a little sheepish.

"Neither, Brad."

"Well, do you measure your conversion rates?"

"Never have," Charlie mumbled.

"Great, there's so much room for improvement to your conversion rates, and I'm going to teach you another 80 or so strategies you can pick from. This is going to be great."

Charlie Meets Adrian the Printer for a Very Powerful Lesson on Boosting His Number of Transactions

As we negotiated the traffic circles in the industrial area that was home to Adrian and his print shop, I was relentlessly stressing the importance of having a detailed database of everyone who comes into contact with one's business.

"You'd be amazed at how many businesses can't even make a special offer to their customers because they simply don't know who they are. It's criminal," I lectured.

Upon arriving at Adrian's business, the first thing we were asked to do was to fill in our details, including date of birth, in a guest book. You see, Adrian doesn't miss a single chance at boosting his incredible database.

When Adrian first contacted *Action International*, he had a typical printer's mentality. "Times are tough," he told us. "But what do you expect with the economy the way it is?" Within 10 seconds, I had gathered that Adrian regularly blamed circumstances out of his control for his own poor performance. I was determined to change that.

After investigating the state of his business, it became clear that he actually had quite a lot of customers, but many were one-timers and precious few did lots of regular work with him. Now, for someone in the printing industry who has everyone's contact details, this track record was crazy, but very similar to that of most people in business.

We set about turning his business around with the single-minded goal of using his old customers to transform his bottom line.

"You wouldn't believe this now, Charlie, but before I got involved with Brad and his team, the only letters I ever sent my past customers were overdue account notices," Adrian said.

"They were the bad old days," I replied with a grin. "Remember how long it took your Coach to convince you to simply send out a letter, with a brochure on the special printing offers for Christmas, to all your past customers thanking them for their business over the past year?"

Adrian was too embarrassed to answer, so I obliged.

"It took over three weeks of haggling before we sat down to write it for him. It cost next to nothing to put together and the postage came to around $700, if I remember correctly."

"Correct," reiterated Adrian.

"And how much business did you get out of it?"

"$24,000," we said simultaneously.

We then both glanced at Charlie, who hadn't said a word. In fact, Charlie hadn't said much all day. However, his various expressions spoke volumes. Right now his mouth was slightly open and he'd forgotten to blink for the last 60 seconds.

We had begun our coaching of Adrian the same way we start with every business owner who has problems increasing the number of transactions from past customers. We hammered away at the importance of keeping in regular contact with everyone on the database *(if you haven't got one, start now)* and the need to constantly offer special deals, because when people are offered a special deal they feel special.

When he finally relented and sent the Christmas offer, his professional life changed forever. From that day on he unlocked a gold mine containing vast wealth. Today he has a fantastic database.

Adrian collects information on customers' families *(including all birthdays)*, their hobbies, and all facets of their business. At special times of the year like Easter and Christmas he sends them a card, and a special offer—but really, really early. Why? So he can share all the wonderful Easter and Christmas cards he can personalize for the customers.

He knows their wedding anniversaries and any other really special dates that warrant a card.

Which printer do you think these people use, religiously? I'll give you one guess! And who do they turn to for ideas and help develop new products that need printing? Why Adrian of course!

And it's not only all his past customers that flock to him with their printing needs. We also instituted a reward system that encourages people to refer him business. Every offer he makes includes a discount or gift offer if they refer a friend or business colleague. As a result this is the only form of marketing he does, and dollar for dollar the results are astonishing.

"Think about it, Charlie. When was the last time you received a letter in the mail thanking you for your business?"

"It's certainly been a while."

"That's exactly why it's so effective. I know it works, but only a precious few put it into practice. It's the best way to increase the number of transactions known to man."

We thanked Adrian, who had already extracted the name of Charlie's wife, her birthday, the names of their kids, and their wedding anniversary.

As we started towards our next "classroom," I had time to give Charlie another quick example of how important it is to keep in contact with clients.

"Where I work there are four hairdressers within walking distance," I began. "Each one relies on repeat business to make any real money, yet only one has ever bothered to take my details.

"Every five weeks they send me a reminder letter that it's time for a cut and if I don't call, they phone to remind me. They also have a loyalty program where every tenth cut is free. See how proactive they are about getting me back?"

I pointed out that this actually costs them relatively little, but it's no contest when it comes to getting my hair cut. I always go back to them.

"It's important to remember that if you don't treat customers in this way, most will leave you for no apparent reason. It's scary stuff when you think about it in those terms," I continued.

"If people are doing business with you simply because it's convenient, then you're risking your livelihood on their whims—and who wants that? To get some control back over your prosperity you must develop a database and use it like Adrian and my hairdresser."

"What about people that just call up for a quote?" Charlie asked.

"Everyone, Charlie. Make sure there's always a script by the phone that ensures that whoever answers asks for the person's details so you can follow up and send them a special offer."

"I've certainly never done that before."

"And that's why it's so powerful; almost nobody does it."

"Almost everyone except me from now on, Brad. I can assure you of that."

"Great. I've got another 60 ways you can get them back more often."

Charlie Gets to Meet Barbara the Mover for a Lesson in Boosting the Average Dollar Sale

We only had two more destinations left, and since Charlie was absorbing the information like a sponge, I decided to finish our excursion in one day. This would also help impress on him the straightforward nature of what it takes to excel in business. It doesn't take months and years to turn a business around. It can be done almost instantly by applying the principles of the chassis.

"Where to now?" asked Charlie enthusiastically, obviously starting to enjoy himself a little more.

"We're off to see Barbara, who runs a moving company," I explained.

I had met Barbara at a networking breakfast and even though I wasn't making a presentation, she knew who I was and had positioned herself next to me as we sat down.

After the pleasantries were out of the way, she came straight to the point.

"Brad, I need your help," I remember her saying.

She went on to explain how tight the margins were thanks to the competition. She complained that even though they were handling plenty of work thanks to good advertising and healthy word of mouth, their profits were remaining stagnant as all the extra work was being done almost at cost.

It was a story I'd heard often.

As we pulled into Barbara's business the first thing that caught our eyes was the line of moving trucks all in the same striking color. As always they were immaculately clean, a true reflection of Barbara's professional ethos.

"Impressive," mused Charlie.

Once inside her office I began the lesson: "Do you remember that fateful networking breakfast where we first met?"

"The seventeenth of July, 1995," she fired quick as a flash.

"Your problem wasn't a lack of work, but the fact you weren't making enough profit out of a pretty sizable turnover."

"That was pretty much it."

After coffee had arrived on that July seventeenth morning, we had done a little brainstorming. I was convinced that with her already robust client base and steady stream of work, there had to be a way of increasing the average dollar sale and thus improving profitability.

After about 10 minutes of throwing ideas around we hit the jackpot. Insurance, a checklist of other products and services, and increased prices.

By offering all her clients insurance for their move the average dollar sale would go up, and since the insurance had a huge margin, profits would increase dramatically. To pump profits even further, we agreed it would be a good idea to have *normal* insurance as well as *premium*. Premium insurance would be like icing on the cake.

We thought of at least another six things to put on a checklist to upsell every single client and most importantly, I finally convinced Barbara to up her prices by 10 percent. Of course this meant we had to redo the quotes and turn them into action plans.

Then came the toughest part.

We had the solution; now it was a matter of getting her sales team members to sell it. Scripts were made up so that all customers were offered insurance. Well maybe not offered—it was more or less sold to them. You see, instead of getting the sales team to ask, "Would you like to take out insurance with that?" to which most would simply say, "No, thank you," they asked "Which would you like, our normal or our premium insurance?" The customer wasn't really given a choice.

By carefully phrasing the question in this way, the customer felt obliged to go with one of the insurance packages—and often it would be premium for the extra peace of mind since they were going to take insurance anyway.

"That one idea changed my thinking about the entire business, Brad. Since then we've added dry cleaning and gardening to our checklist of services. They all help add value to the customer's experience and as result our average dollar sale and subsequent profits are terrific," Barbara said.

"Oh and the price rise—once we trained the sales team, no one even questioned it. Now on the same turnover, we make about five times as much profit."

"Maybe it's time I thought about offering a few extra products and services," Charlie thought aloud.

"And don't forget to think about how you ask customers if they want them," added Barbara. "What made the insurance idea so successful was the way it was presented," she concluded as we waved good-bye.

No longer dumbstruck by the simplicity of the success stories he was witnessing firsthand, Charlie began appreciating the possibility that their success could also be his. He was beginning to see that the principles of the chassis applied to all businesses, no matter what industry they were in.

He was beginning to see the light.

"I'm starting to realize how this could work for me, Brad," he said as we fastened our seat belts. "And I've got to admit that I'm excited and angry both at the same time."

"Why angry?" I asked.

"Because I should have known about this 20 years ago when I first started the business."

"I can coach you in another 50 or so ways to boost your average dollar sale, so that anger will soon be replaced with extra profits," I assured him as we left for our final stop.

Charlie Meets Ryan, the Sporting Goods Retailer, for a Lesson on Boosting Margins

I couldn't wait to catch up with Ryan again. He had been referred to *Action* by a friend and our tutelage started with a fair amount of skepticism on his part. We soon began making some great breakthroughs, particularly in the area of improving margins, and that was why Charlie was here.

"Good afternoon, Brad," he yelled from the tennis clothes section as we entered his shop.

I introduced him to Charlie, who was eyeing a handsome FILA polo shirt. "Why not take a look at the new Reebok line, Charlie," offered Ryan as he led him towards the brightly colored shirts.

"I'll bet you a hundred dollars that you're making a better margin on those Reebok shirts than the FILAs," I said.

"Now hang on a minute," was all he could manage as we burst out laughing.

When focusing on the last part of the chassis, it was Ryan's huge range of products that meant we had to always try and focus the customer's attention on the product with the highest margin.

The way we did this was to cut back on his sales teams members' basic salary and then increase their commission. The really important part, and frankly the one that made it work, was tying their commissions to the margin of the product they were selling. In effect, they would get a percentage of the margin instead of the overall sale.

Do you think this made them focus on the higher-margin products? Of course, it did, and as a result, while the turnover of the business remained relatively stable, profits went north.

"You told me, Ryan, that the most important part of making it work was open communication with team members," I said.

"Absolutely, Brad. It all hinged on being able to relay to every team member what we were doing and why. Everyone knows exactly what the margins are and what they need to do to make the best money. If you don't spell it out very clearly, you can't hope to make a system like this work."

The real beauty for Ryan is that during quiet times, he isn't burdened by high salaries, as wages are directly linked to how much is being sold. It's the safest way to run a business: pay on performance. It's also a great motivator offering tremendous opportunity for those who can sell.

We also took a hard look at the cost side of the business. I was convinced we could cut at least 10 percent from his overheads. And once again we got the team involved.

"Getting the team behind the cost cutting was the real key," confirmed Ryan. "We sat down together and individually identified all the areas we could work on. Then I declared that all the money saved would go into a pool with 50 percent going to the bottom line and the other half going towards an end-of-year party that everyone would enjoy.

"It didn't take long before people were getting right behind the effort. We ended up saving so much that all team members and their partners stayed in the mountains for the weekend, all expenses paid. Naturally, it was also great for my own profits."

Some of the savings achieved were simple yet significant, like ordering all stationery only once during the week from one of the big suppliers. Other ideas were a little more creative. The office administrator warmed to the challenge of cutting costs and she recommended purchasing software that would allow faxes to be sent directly from the computer in the middle of the night.

Because Ryan's business sent thousands of faxes a year, often to overseas suppliers, the company saved a fortune using this technology to take advantage of off-peak national and international phone rates.

"It was amazing how enthusiastically cost cutting was embraced when there was something in it for the team members," remembered Ryan.

"What do you reckon, Charlie? Have you seen enough?" I asked.

"Plenty, Brad. Plenty."

I mentioned that I would have one of my Coaches show him the other 60 ways to improve his margins, and his excitement turned to sheer desire to get back to work.

The Drive Home

We thanked Ryan and drove off as the sun was setting on a big day for my friend. I don't think he'd ever had so much to think about before.

"What I've shown you today, Charlie, is only the tip of the iceberg. All you've seen is a few examples of how each area of the Business Chassis works."

"Yeah, but that's more than I've ever been exposed to in the past. I think my head is going to explode."

"Trust me, it won't. I decided to show you these strategies in *Action* so you could appreciate the reality of their success. It's not just theory or my saying they work; it's happening out there right now. However, as with anything of this nature, people know it works but only a select few have the initiative to put these strategies into practice. That's why I'm going to insist you get a Coach."

"I think that's a great idea, Brad."

"I want you to make a real commitment to carry through with what I've shown you. You know it works, don't you?"

"Sure, I've seen it."

"Then you must stop at nothing before it's working for you. You've got to stop just wanting success and start making it happen."

"You have my commitment, Brad."

"Excellent," I said loudly as we pulled up in front of his garage.

"Today I've given you the inspiration to go forward and now I've given you the practical tools that will make it virtually impossible for you to break that commitment you've just made."

Charlie looked at me quizzically as I pulled out a thickish folder.

"In here you'll find over 250 no-nonsense ways in which you could boost every part of your Business Chassis."

"250!" he said, startled.

"Not every tip will apply to you, but there are so many to choose from that making the gains we talked about earlier when I first introduced you to the chassis is well within your reach. With this document there are *no excuses*.

"And, what's more your *Action* Coach will show you how to make every single one of them work in your business, and they'll make sure you keep that commitment.

"Charlie, one last thing."

"Yes, Brad."

"I want you to play this board game at least a half dozen times before your Coach calls you next week."

"*'Leverage'*—What's it all about?" he asked.

"Just play it. It'll really teach you about making money from your business."

Charlie took the game and the folder and with a firm handshake the lesson was over.

I now offer this folder to you. In Part 4 you'll find every tip I gave to Charlie, and it's the same deal. And, when you're ready, call my team and get your copy of *"Leverage,"* the board game. Now *you* have *no excuses* either. Success is yours for the taking.

$$\boxed{\textbf{Part 4}}$$

∎ 282 Tips to Make It Happen

Before we get into this, I'd like to first outline how you can use this section to develop a custom-made marketing plan that is guaranteed to pump up your business.

Ideally, as you work through the pages that follow, you should aim to select five ideas for each of the five parts of the Business Chassis. That will give you 25 ideas to get started with. Imagine that—in a couple of hours you will have 25 proven, powerful marketing ideas that you can instantly put to use.

Do the relevant surveys, if you need to, and then fill in the forms for your *Five Killer Strategies* for each part of the Business Chassis. When you've completed all five killer strategy forms, they add together to become your marketing plan.

And that's really only the beginning. Once you've applied those 25, why not choose another 25? Of course, if you were to start another business, this book will prove just as useful all over again.

After working out which strategies you'd like to try, go straight to the action plan form at the end of the book and fill out one for each element of the Business Chassis. This is where you make the commitment to really give the ideas your best shot. You work out when you're going to get started, how much implementing the idea will cost, how many extra sales you'll need to break even, and when your testing period will finish.

Once you've tested these 25 ideas, you should find you have at least 10 worth hanging onto and running again. That also means you'll find a number that didn't do anything for your business and cost you money. But that's just part of the game. It's really only a small price to pay for a stack of ideas that actually do work and that you can run forever.

You might be surprised at how much going through an exercise like this will reveal about your business. It may get you thinking about important issues that have never before crossed your mind. If much of this information is new to you, don't be concerned. There's never been a better time to start getting some real results from your business.

Make sure you make notes as you progress through the book. That way, when you come to writing your first few strategies, you'll find it much easier.

Now it's time to get started—there's so much business out there to be had. It's just up to you to get out there and claim it.

Leads

This is definitely the most thought-about area of marketing, and obviously the most glamorous. Most businesspeople invest, or should I say *waste* more money trying to get potential customers than they do in any other area of marketing.

Running an advertisement is easy; after all there are enough salespeople constantly calling you with offers of airtime or space so all you need to do is say "Yes." Hey, they'll even write the ad for you. And, you guessed it, I'm being sarcastic when I say they're brilliant at writing ads to help you sell things.

By the way, if you want to learn more about how to write ads, read my other book, *Instant Advertising.*

But to start the money flowing, let's go through all the different strategies you can use to bring new prospects to your business. And, just to make sure you focus on doing what works, I'll give you my hints, tips, and ratings on each one.

Remember, the ratings indicate *value* for money spent. Ideas with a rating of 2/5 might bring a better response *(in pure number terms)* than something rated 4/5, but because it's more expensive, the acquisition cost of each sale skyrockets.

Perfect examples are the first two tips in this chapter. Local newspaper advertising gets 4/5 while advertising in one of the big dailies gets only 3/5. That's because, dollar for dollar, the local paper offers better value.

If you want to make a sale, you've first got to generate leads. And if you want to increase the amount of business you do, you need to increase the number of leads you generate. You need to get more people to visit your business with the view to buying from you.

But how will you know you've been able to increase the amount of leads you get if you don't know how many you are getting right now? I find it very interesting that when I ask most businesspeople how many leads they get each week, they say they don't know. They simply have no idea what methods work for them and what don't.

The first thing you need to do is to start measuring the number of leads you're getting. Start by asking people who come into your business or phone in where they heard about you. And keep records.

Start doing this *right now*. I can't stress this enough. If there's one thing I tell business owners when consulting with them, it's this: If you don't know what's working and what's not, you can't possibly make informed decisions.

And you'll never know which ads to run. You may keep running an ad that never results in a sale.

Customers usually come from many different sources, making it difficult to judge how an ad is working from sales results alone. It could be that you simply received more referrals that week.

You need to find out for sure. Create a tally sheet and include all the possible ways people could hear about you. These could include newspaper ads, television ads, radio ads, referrals, direct mail, flyers, Yellow Pages, or walk-bys.

Every time someone buys, ask the question, "By the way, can I ask where you heard about my business?" Nobody, and I mean nobody, will have a problem telling you. Make a mark on the tally sheet in the relevant column. Keep at it and ensure that everyone on your team does the same. Then, after two weeks or a month, tally up and get the figures.

You'll then have a far better idea of where your leads are coming from. And you'll know exactly how many you are getting each day and week of the month. You might even be surprised at what this simple exercise tells you.

Here's an example of a tally sheet:

LEADS SURVEY

Start Date: _____

End Date: _____

Name of Team Member: _____

SOURCE

Regular Customer: _____

TV: _____

Radio: _____

Daily Newspaper: _____

Local Newspaper: _____

Referral: _____

Direct Mail: _____

Flyer: _____

Yellow Pages: _____

Walk-By: _____

Other: _____

You should measure your leads before you begin developing your instant marketing plan, and of course, you should continually remeasure as an ongoing exercise so you can fine-tune, refocus, modify, or repeat strategies. But more on that later.

Now it's time to begin developing your instant marketing plan. Having completed the initial Leads Survey, you'll have a very good idea of where your leads are currently coming from. You could decide to implement strategies to complement trends picked up through this survey. For instance, if you are getting most leads from existing local newspaper ads, you may decide to stick with this basic strategy by increasing your advertising frequency (but with better ads), and to increase your reach by including daily newspapers and radio advertising as well. Or, you could choose to try a different approach by trying mailbox drops and direct mail in addition to newspaper advertising for the first time.

60 TIPS FOR GENERATING MORE LEADS
Local Newspaper Advertising

These papers are usually weekly, and distributed free to the local area. They are becoming more popular as we adopt a far more local or regional focus. Radio, TV, and the Internet can instantly bring you the world news, so the local newspaper is becoming more focused on events in a certain area, and these weekly papers allow even more interaction between the readers and their paper.

It really can be a cost-effective way to reach your local market, especially homemakers. The rates are generally affordable, as the paper has a shelf life of at least a week. 90 percent of results come in the first four days, but results will still come in up to six weeks after delivery.

Hints and Tips:

1. Get on an early right-hand page.

2. Design the ad yourself with a benefit-oriented headline.

3. Don't use your company name in the headline.

4. Make an offer that people have to respond to—a call to action.

5. Don't be afraid to haggle on price—often these publications will negotiate on rates.

6. Remember that *potential* readership and *actual* are two totally different numbers.

7. Test and measure your headlines and placements.

Rating: 4/5

Daily Newspapers

This is your major daily, that is, the city paper read by most people. These papers come out daily, and are generally read by people on their way to work, or people interested in keeping up-to-date with world events. They can be expensive, so you need to make sure your product appeals to a wide group of people in order to make it cost effective.

Usually 90 percent of your results come within 48 hours. It's best to test and measure which day of the week works best for you. Usually Saturday and Sunday papers outperform the weekday papers. A good rainy day on Sunday will always boost response. Also, remember to test the section you advertise in.

Hints and Tips:

1. Use an early right-hand page (pay extra if you have to).

2. Target your headline to the type of customer you want.

3. Use a good picture and write an advertorial.

4. Test and measure your offers.

Rating: 3/5

Television Advertising

Usually best suited for products or services with mass appeal and high distribution. Because the ad will be seen by people from diverse demographics and a large geographical area, it needs to be available widely, or accessible by most. Try and add a direct response element, to make it measurable. Image-building TV ads that are not for small business—make yours sell. Consider carefully before going into TV, but don't automatically rule yourself out.

There are many companies that have gone on advertorial style programs and, for an outlay of under $5000, have received three or four minutes of air time. That's quite a big sum for many small businesses, but you get a national TV audience for a period of time that really allows you to sell the benefits of your product. It's worked wonders for some, but you need to have a toll-free number and enough people manning the phones to accommodate the flood of calls right after you go on air. It's no good having two lines and hoping they will keep ringing for three days. It happens fast!

Look at it from a financial perspective. How many sales will you need to generate to cover your investment?

Hints and Tips:

1. Your schedule is the key; only advertise when your target is watching.

2. Make sure people know how to get what you're selling.

3. Use the company's name several times and the phone number at least twice for a minimum of five seconds.

4. Make an offer that people have to respond to.

5. Test and measure your schedule on different channels.

Rating: 4/5, but only if the product has mass appeal

Radio Advertising

A cheap medium that's best for products with immediacy. Also good as support for TV. Bear in mind that people don't usually actively listen to the radio. It's a background medium, so your ad must really leap out and speak to *them*. Best for products and services where people can take advantage of an advertised offer within the next 24 hours. It's the last advertising medium heard before shopping.

Radio is also great to promote or remind people of an already well-promoted event. Use it to ask for a direct response, and get people to call in now.

Hints and Tips:

1. The time of day, or simply put, your schedule, is the key to your success. Breakfast and drive time are the most listened to programs, so pay the extra.

2. Make sure your ad *sells*.

3. Give people an easy way to respond.

4. Make an offer that people have to respond to.

5. Test and measure different ads.

Rating: 4/5

Magazine Advertising

A great way to go after a very specific target market. It's usually pretty easy to judge who is reading a magazine by the types of articles, as well as the other advertisers. People reading magazines will pay attention to the ads, as the ads generally represent their direct interest. The challenge is that your competitors will be there too.

Check the cost effectiveness, as some smaller magazines will ask you to spend a lot to get to only very few—but if it's your target market it may be worth it.

Hints and Tips:

1. Get on an early right-hand page.

2. Make sure your ad fits the style of the magazine.

3. Use a powerful photo of people using your product or service.

4. Make an offer that people have to respond to.

5. Test and measure different ads, offers, and magazines.

Rating: 3/5

Trade Journal Advertising

Excellent for reaching a very particular group of professionals or businesspeople. As with magazine advertising, your competitors will also be there, but people will take the time to read and evaluate. Can be extremely cost-effective and great for industry profile.

Hints and Tips:

1. Write more of an article than an advertisement.

2. Build credibility for yourself and your product.

3. Make an offer that people have to respond to.

Rating: 3/5

Industry Newsletter Ads

These newsletters are sent to very particular people, and advertising in them can be effective. The challenge can be the low interest people take—if they haven't paid for the newsletter, they may not read it properly. In fact, they may not even get to the page your ad is on. Therefore, pay special attention to whether people read the newsletter or not.

It may pay to buy the list of recipients and direct mail them rather than just advertise in the newsletter.

Hints and Tips:

1. Do your homework on who gets and reads it.

2. Build credibility through an advertorial.

3. Make an offer that people have to respond to.

4. Test and measure different newsletters.

Rating: 3/5

School Newsletter Ads

Generally very cheap. There's also the benefit of appearing as though you're in part *endorsed* by the school, adding credibility and trust. Excellent for stationery, educational products, and so forth. These newsletters are read, although not intensely.

Hints and Tips:

1. Make sure you're targeting the right audience.

2. Make an offer that people have to respond to.

3. Test and measure your headlines and offers.

Rating: 5/5

Inserts

This is where you arrange for a flyer to be inserted into a newspaper or magazine. These can work well, as they literally fall out at the readers' feet. The problem is, their next stop is generally the trash. You need to work on your headline, so that people stop and read. On the plus side, people *will* see your ad. The only thing to look out for is multiple inserts. If there will be other inserts along with yours, most people dump the lot in the trash as soon as possible. Try and make sure you are the only one.

Hints and Tips:

1. The bulkier your insert the better chance of readership.

2. Make it high quality and gimmicky.

3. Make an offer that people have to respond to.

4. Test and measure.

Rating: 2/5

Press Releases

This is where you fax, send, or e-mail media outlets a story on your business and encourage them to publish it as free advertising. They will do this only if first, there is a newsworthy angle to your article, and second, that it is well written and almost "print ready." Journalists have to fill so much space every day/week/month—if you make their job easy and give them a good story, they'll consider publishing it. The best way is to call first, and say, "I'm just faxing through a really good idea for a story," then fax it. Follow up afterwards.

Have a good photo ready to send if requested (if you're only mailing a few, send a photo with the letter), and make sure you include all your contact details so you can be reached 24 hours a day.

Because journalists get so many press releases every day, it's vital to make it as newsworthy as possible. Forget about what you think is important and instead put yourself in the shoes of the readers/viewers/listeners. If your story is likely to grab these people's attention, then you're more likely to grab the journalist's attention.

Hints and Tips:

1. It's not what you know but *who*. You need to do some research.

2. Write like a journalist, not an advertiser.

3. Do it all the time and build a profile for yourself.

4. See if you can write a regular column or be a regular contributor.

5. Test and measure what you send and whom you send it to.

Rating: 5/5

Mailbox Drops

A cheap medium, but an unreliable one. Most flyers get dumped in the trash without a real look. Your headline must speak to the readers right away, and offer them something very attractive. People are starting to resent junk mail, and will only respond to flyers that speak to them directly. Good for local businesses, and especially fast-food and home-delivery businesses.

You've got to be gimmicky to stand out, and remember quality. Larger catalogs seem to be kept and read.

Hints and Tips:

1. Go either full quality or really cheap, not half and half.

2. Make sure they actually get delivered.

3. Make a great offer. Attach something so it stands out from the rest.

4. Determine which areas respond the best and then do them regularly.

5. Test and measure with a few thousand first.

Rating: 3/5

Sidewalk Handbills

That is, handing out flyers on the street. This can be good if you have an incredible offer, and your business is just a quick walk from where you are handing out the flyers. Most people dump them immediately, so again, you must reach the target market. The benefit is that you can pick and choose whom you hand the flyers to—whether it's women, young people, or a group more specific still.

Hints and Tips:

1. Have an attractive person handing them out with something that adds excitement (sorry if that sounds shallow, but it's reality).

2. Make it simple so you can immediately see the benefit.

3. Make a great offer that people have to respond to.

4. Test and measure where and when you hand them out.

Rating: 4/5

Catalogs

Can be used to mail out to your existing customers, to hand out in store, or to use as a mailbox drop. Works when you have numerous different product categories, and lots of specials. The front page should offer reasons for the prospect to look inside. Use teasers like "Inside...how you can save $45 on a new DVD player," etc. Not recommended for the average small business as a lead generation technique.

Hints and Tips:

1. Should only be used by big companies who have wholesalers and manufacturers ready to help pay for them.

2. Use them as sales tools or repeat business catalysts, not lead generators.

3. Test and measure.

Rating: 2/5

Brochures

Best used as a sales aid. Unless your brochure contains compelling headlines, most people will generally look at the pictures then throw the brochure away. Of course, it depends upon the situation. In the case where the decision is a big one (car, home, major electrical, investment, etc.), a brochure can be just the sort of backup you need during the sales process. People will often hang onto a brochure for a long time, so it's worth making it attractive and glossy. However, don't make the mistake of relying on your brochure to sell—it's only an aid.

Hints and Tips:

1. Use to help you sell, not to generate leads.

2. Invest in glossy paper, as people are likely to keep it a while.

3. Test and measure.

Rating: 1/5

Yellow Pages

Excellent for some products, especially the types that people buy only occasionally. Yellow Pages will work for you as long as you realize statistics show that more than 35 percent of people turn to the Yellow Pages when they're ready to buy. Also their own statistics show response increases with an increase in ad size, or Unit Display (UD) size. The increase in responses is one for a 1UD, four for a 2UD, seven for a 3UD, and eleven for a 4UD. Therefore, the bigger the better.

The important thing is to stand out. Do something different than what everyone else is doing, and remember that your readers are already buyers; they're just deciding who they should buy from and, in general, they will call three advertisers before making a decision. Remember, you can advertise in more than just your local Yellow Pages.

Hints and Tips:

1. Run a benefit-filled headline.

2. Use a photo rather than a line drawing.

3. Use key words so people know what you do.

4. Make sure your phone number is big and in the bottom right-hand corner.

5. Test and measure. Use a sales script to answer the calls.

Rating: 5/5

White Pages

White Pages are often underrated by businesses. Of course, you can't advertise, but it's important that people can find you. You may want to go for a bold heading so you're easily seen. If you're doing radio, there's no harm in adding the line "Find us under 'V' in the White Pages" to your script. Also remember the White Pages are available across the whole country; it could be an idea to put yourself in all of them.

Hints and Tips:

1. Use **BOLD** so you stand out.

2. Make sure you list as many numbers as you can and in as many directories as you need to.

Rating: 4/5

Other Directories

Other phone directories are generally a risky proposition, as the Yellow Pages are so established as the standard. Before deciding on another directory, see if you can find out how it works for people who are currently advertising. Also, think about how many sales you need to make in order to pay for the listing. If it's a reasonable gamble, take it. One last thing: If you're going to use another directory, remember that the rules of advertising in the Yellow Pages apply.

Hints and Tips:

1. Call several current advertisers and get feedback.

2. Set the ad yourself with a benefit-oriented headline.

3. Check how much promotion they do to get people using the directory.

4. See if you're going to be the only player in your section.

Rating: 3/5

Barter-and-Trade Exchanges

These can be an excellent way to score customers you wouldn't have otherwise attracted. People will come to you just because you're a member of the trade exchange, and they'll be less obsessed with price and other buying criteria. Again, investigate a little first and ask for references. Just remember, only ever take a small percentage of your business on trade or you could run out of cash.

Hints and Tips:

1. Make sure you have enough profit margin to use trade.

2. Be proactive; don't wait for business to come to you.

3. Take trade dollars when you'd usually have downtime and cash buyers aren't around.

4. It can drive you broke if you don't watch yourself.

5. Test and measure.

Rating: 3/5

Buy Database Lists

You buy a list of names from a list broker. The lists can be very specific, and you may find what you're looking for. Be careful, though—some lists are very poor quality, so ask questions. How were the names compiled? How old is the list? How many people have mailed to it? How did they do? Can you talk to them? Do they offer guarantees? Can you test 200 names at random?

Your letter needs to be punchy and offer something people can respond to right away. It's a great way to access people you wouldn't normally reach.

One last thing: You can now subscribe to database services, or even buy CD-ROMs with every business on disk. The White Pages, for instance, have every listed business on CD.

Hints and Tips:

1. The quality of the list is imperative.

2. Make sure your letter *sells*.

3. Remember, these people don't know you.

4. Make an offer that people have to respond to.

5. Test and measure different lists and letters.

Rating: 4/5

DIY Direct Mail

Write a letter to a list you compile yourself, either from the Yellow Pages or another kind of directory. It pays to include a gimmick with the letter, something to help people remember it, and always follow the letter with a phone call.

Direct mail is by far the most cost-effective advertising medium, as it goes directly into the hands of your target. If you know all of the people you're selling to, don't just cold call. Send them a letter that gets them excited and then promise to call them. Telephone follow-up increases response by up to 300 percent.

Hints and Tips:

1. Your first 50 words are your headline, make them *sell*.

2. Your P.S. is the most powerful seller. Use it.

3. Write as if you are speaking to someone, *not* in the old proper formal letter style.

4. Tell them what you're going to tell them, tell them, and then tell them what you told them. Follow up on the phone.

5. Use exciting, stimulating words to describe everything.

6. Test and measure headlines and offers.

Rating: 5/5

Piggyback Invoice Mailings

If you're friendly with other business owners, why not ask if you can include a flyer or letter with their regular invoice mailings? You could offer to pay for the mailout as an incentive, but remember, you don't have to. You could even ask if they will write (or simply sign) a letter recommending your services.

This works brilliantly when noncompeting companies with the same target market work together.

Hints and Tips:

1. Have a great offer that's just for their customers.

2. Make a *free* offer so the other business gets the credit.

3. It should sound as though this great offer is possible only because your two companies are working together.

4. Test and measure.

Rating: 4/5

Tender Lists

If you're in an industry where you get a lot of tenders or bids for projects, you can buy or subscribe to tender publications that let you know of every tender or project coming to the market. Usually they're full of great work, but often they're too far behind the times for you to get a good tender in on time.

The best list is the industry grapevine; make sure you get in on it. By the way, when you are submitting tenders or bids, be sure to make it a sales document rather than just a typical tender document. This will really make you stand out.

Hints and Tips:

1. Ask for a month's trial to see how good the list is.

2. Call everyone who has a tender or project that may interest you.

3. Get tenders or bids in *on* time.

4. Test and measure.

Rating: 3/5

Faxes

These can work well, but are often seen as intrusions. Fortunately, however, if the fax is well targeted, and better still, addressed to someone (or at least a position), there's a chance it will succeed. It's really worth the time researching the person's name that should receive it.

A phone follow-up makes it more effective still. You can also do the mystery fax idea—that is, send a fax addressed to no one. The person who picks it up will take it to everyone and ask, "Is this yours?" This ensures that everyone will see it.

Hints and Tips:

1. Make sure it's got a great headline.

2. Use a company specializing in faxes, so they take care of everything.

3. Give everything a sense of urgency.

4. Test and measure.

Rating: 4/5

Billboards and Posters

These are excellent as a directional medium. That means you use the billboard to tell people to take the next left, or that you're five minutes away. Why do you think the big fast-food chains use billboards all the time?

It's also a good way to support other media, especially TV and radio. Your product should have wide appeal and be simple to understand.

It's also a great way of promoting a product you might sell through retailers. It's a far less direct response medium than many others, so ask people to respond.

Hints and Tips:

1. Great picture, and short, simple headline.

2. Easy response instructions, short and sweet.

3. Test and measure different boards and places.

Rating: 3/5

Coupons

Advertising on the back of supermarket receipts can work if your ad includes a coupon that people will want to collect. If your business has mass appeal and is local, it can be very effective, especially if your prices appeal to the local "coupon cutters." Generally works best for lower-priced products and services.

Hints and Tips:

1. Make a great offer that people simply can't refuse.

2. Make it plain and simple as to what you're offering.

3. Give it value so people want to keep it.

4. Make sure it's local.

5. Test and measure.

Rating: 3/5

Backs of Taxis and Sides of Buses

This is a fairly obscure way to market yourself. Good for event promotion and public announcement advertising. Also good for product awareness, but usually poor for direct response. Should only really be considered if you've done most other suitable things, or you get a great deal.

Hints and Tips:

1. Same principles as billboards.

2. Make it attract the eye and attention.

3. Test and measure.

Rating: 2/5

Cinema Advertising

There are two types: still and moving. Still is where you display a still frame, while the announcer reads a script. Moving is where you have a TV commercial playing. As a rule, people do not watch the still, but do watch the moving. Moving commercials in the cinema are generally used only by advertisers with a high budget. Still commercials are generally used by local businesses. If you're going to try it, make sure you write the script and that it speaks directly to the people you want to target. Make them an offer to come in. Incidentally, cinema can be a good way to reach people between the ages of 18 and 30. However, it's something you should leave until last on your promotion list.

Hints and Tips:

1. Use a picture with impact that grabs and holds attention.

2. Write a script that speaks directly to the viewer.

3. Test and measure.

Rating: 0/5

Sponsorships

Generally quite a passive marketing tool, depending on how you use it. Sponsoring sports teams can work well if you get a good profile, or naming rights. It's mostly an awareness-building tool, which can mean it has questionable cost effectiveness. If you sponsor local clubs or teams, make sure they allow you to have a list of all members of the club, so you can mail to them. Once again, just an image-building exercise that may or may not work in the long run.

Hints and Tips:

1. Do it because you think it will work, not just to donate your money.

2. Make sure you're reaching your target audience.

3. Find a way to directly contact your prospects.

4. Test and measure.

Rating: 1/5

Postcard Mailings

This is where you send prospects a postcard that advertises your business. It is similar to direct mail or flyers, although there are other benefits. The first is that postcards make for an ideal *teaser*—that is, they don't tell you the whole story. For example, send a postcard that says: "In two days, someone will call to help double the value of your investments."

It's also great to use a wonderful photo and a simple sales message.

Hints and Tips:

1. Target your audience well.

2. Make your picture(s) stand out and grab attention.

3. Make sure it *sells*, and give them a way to respond.

4. Make an offer or even just print a gift check that people can bring in and spend with you.

Rating: 4/5

Internet/Web Pages

This is an area that changes every day. Anything written about the Internet today will be out-of-date tomorrow. As a general rule, remember that the Internet is a worldwide medium, and most people still aren't using it. But, this is changing. The Internet is good for complex products, big-decision products to generate leads, software, music, travel, and other commodity-type products that people don't need to touch and feel before purchasing. Remember, people use the "Net" to research a purchase, so a Web page is a must.

Hints and Tips:

1. Can work well if you're selling a commodity product.

2. Make sure you submit your site to all the different search engines often.

3. Make it easy to download and navigate. Keep big files and pictures to a minimum, as they can take too long to download.

4. Fill your site with interesting information. This is why people will visit you in the first place.

5. Budget wisely. Internet site design costs have a habit of getting out of hand.

Rating: 4/5

Building Signage

In many cases, this will be your most important form of advertising. This especially applies to fast-food restaurants and businesses with high-roadside visibility. Make the signage work for you—offer benefits and good deals. Instead of "Computer Upgrades," try something like "Upgrade your old computer for less than $500 here!"

Hints and Tips:

1. Make the sign bright and colorful.

2. If possible have the same sign facing in two directions so traffic heading each way can see it.

3. Write it so it *sells*. Include your best headline.

4. Focus on benefits, not features.

Rating: 5/5

Car Signage

Often used by network marketers, and almost never works for them. However, an argument for it is that your car is an advertising medium you own. After all, if you don't have to pay for it, there's no real gamble, is there?

Hints and Tips:

1. Don't try to say too much—keep it simple.

2. Think of it as a billboard and use the same sorts of *selling* words.

3. Be bold and different with your use of colors and graphics.

4. Use your phone numbers.

Rating: 4/5

In-Store and Sidewalk Signage

As with building signage, this can be your most powerful form of advertising. This applies especially if you're in a shopping center or strip mall. Using an "A-Frame" with a good headline and an arrow can work. Include an offer—something like "3-day offer...come in for your FREE 15-minute minifacial."

Hints and Tips:

1. Grab people with a catchy headline.

2. Include a special offer that forces people to investigate further.

3. Use catchy fonts and colors.

4. Test and measure.

Rating: 4/5

Window Displays

You'll find people will look at displays, often because they are bored, but mainly because there is no one there to put any pressure on them. They can look for as long as they want without being harassed. This is why real estate windows work so well, and always tend to attract a large number of lookers. Do something interesting, and encourage people to come in with "More Inside" or "Come in to try on this suit in your size."

Hints and Tips:

1. Your top priority is getting people inside so you can make an offer they can't refuse.

2. Change it regularly to keep people's interest.

3. Think of it as a billboard, not just something to decorate.

4. Display the product that has the most mass appeal.

5. Test and measure.

Rating: 4/5

Shopping Center Promotions

Generally cost-effective, as it gets your name advertised directly to people who are already in the center. You can offer the shopping center something to give away as a prize in a competition. This will certainly raise your profile.

Hints and Tips:

1. Make sure you're situated in the busiest part of the center.

2. Check that there aren't competitors right next to you.

3. Work with management and other shopkeepers on ways to help promote your presence.

4. Make it easy for people to buy (credit card facilities are a must), as almost every purchase will be impulse.

5. Test and measure.

Rating: 3/5

Create an Industry Newsletter

Why not make your own newsletter that you send to every person in the industry? Write the articles about your business, but write them as though the newsletter is genuine. It will eventually be picked up and read by the right people. And why not include gossip, pictures, and readers' letters? You then have full reign to advertise your product wherever you want, and how you want. You can also have mock editorial content recommending your business. You could even branch out and sell advertising space to other noncompetitive businesses.

Hints and Tips:

1. The information must be of general interest to your target market.

2. Make it a quarterly, bimonthly, or monthly. Either way, stick to deadlines so people start expecting it.

3. To be respected you must look professional, so invest the time and money in professional layout and photography. It's better to leave out a photo than include a bad one just for the sake of it.

4. Spend a large portion of your time making the cover as striking as possible.

5. Test and measure.

Rating: 3/5

Stickers and Tags

Stickers and tags are great ways to advertise a business where the product is bought irregularly and is fairly unimportant to the buyer. For example, with a printer cartridge supply company, people don't really mind where they buy from, as long as it's quick, cheap, and easy. By placing a sticker on the printer, they'll always call you when they need a cartridge. The best way is to go door-to-door with the stickers, or mail them to people with a cover letter.

Hints and Tips:

1. Use bright colors and a catchy design.

2. Include a photo or logo.

3. Explain clearly what you do.

4. Include all possible forms of contact, as the sticker might still be around after you've changed address.

5. Test and measure.

Rating: 5/5

Fridge Magnets

Again, a good idea for businesses that are only required rarely, such as plumbers or electricians. Can also work for fast-food outlets and restaurants.

Bear in mind that people often forget about your fridge magnet and go to the Yellow Pages anyway. The magnet can easily lose its impact. Joint fridge magnets can work well, that is, magnets advertising a range of local businesses. These are generally held onto.

Hints and Tips:

1. All points mentioned above for stickers and tags are relevant here as well.

2. Try to join forces with other noncompeting businesses. That way it becomes a much more valuable list.

3. Should be hand delivered to the local area.

Rating: 4/5

Named Promotional Gifts

A risky proposition. This is where you have pens designed with your logo on them, or something similar. The gift could be as large as a set of golf clubs. Ideally, the gift should be useful and of quality. This idea is probably better put to use in order to keep your existing customers happy.

Hints and Tips:

1. Go for something a little different—not another coffee mug.

2. Ensure that it's of high quality, as it is a reflection of your business.

3. Personalize it.

Rating: 2/5

Blimps, Plane Banners, and Skywriting

Very high profile, and guaranteed to get people looking, and talking. Of course, it's only suitable for large businesses, and generally only works as an awareness builder. It can work very well in the case of a special event, such as, "Toyota closeout sale ends in 3 days. Hurry!"

Hints and Tips:

1. Only for *very* special events.

2. Of little value if you haven't already got brand awareness.

3. Test and measure.

Rating: 0/5

Business Cards

Highly overrated as a marketing tool. You're better off funneling your money into something more marketing orientated. People will only hang onto your business cards if you give them a reason to do so in the first place. Even so, it pays to put more than just your "name, rank, and serial number" on the cards. Try adding some benefits, and your main point of difference.

Hints and Tips:

1. Include what you *do* and some benefits.

2. Be creative with colors and layout.

3. Give people a reason to hang onto the card.

4. Use the back to explain your company's services or history.

5. Test and measure. Just hand them to everyone.

Rating: 2/5

Networking Functions

Can be extremely effective. People buy from people they like, know, and trust. If you get to know people on a social basis, they are more likely to do business with you. This method can outstrip every other method if done right. You need the right mix of genuine friendliness and salesmanship. That is, don't be too pushy, but be pushy enough. Make it easy for the other person, and follow up!

Hints and Tips:

1. Be friendly and positive.

2. Have some information on your business handy for those interested.

3. Spend more time listening than speaking, as this will endear you to others, and be sure to collect their business cards.

4. Make sure you follow up any interest with a phone call within two days.

5. Test and measure.

Rating: 5/5

Salespeople and Cold Calling

Hiring more salespeople can be one of the smartest things you'll ever do. The most important consideration is "will all sales reps pay for themselves?" Offering a low base salary and a generous commission is the ideal way to ensure that. If they sell a little, you break even. If they sell a lot, you do well. And of course, you can always put them on trial, letting them go if they don't work out.

Hints and Tips:

1. Give salespeople *big* incentives to perform.

2. Look at salespeople as investments, not expenses.

3. Make sure they aren't burdened with paperwork. Keep them focused.

4. Continually motivate by rewarding success—and helping people reach success.

5. Test and measure. Set goals and performance standards.

Rating: 4/5

Telemarketing

This is a great way to set appointments and get new customers. Be sure you are calling a qualified list that will be interested. Get top people who sound friendly and relaxed on the phone. And give them a great script that hooks people.

Excellent if you have an incredibly good offer in stock that you want to move quickly, or to get into a company where you've had trouble selling face-to-face.

Hints and Tips:

1. Make sure you have good lists.

2. Use experienced telemarketers.

3. Ensure that you have a great script that includes a wonderful offer.

4. Test and measure both scripts and offers.

Rating: 5/5

Competitions

Usually done in conjunction with another business, although it can be done outside your store or through advertising. The best thing is that you get to compile a list of names of people who are interested. After the competition, it's best to write them a letter telling them who won, and that you've got a special offer as a consolation prize. Works well when you have a product most people would love to have but don't think they need. Of course, your competition prize could be something other than your product, but that will be less effective in attracting the right sort of people.

Hints and Tips:

1. Make sure you get people's contact details.

2. Use one of your own products as the prize so you get some general recognition.

3. Make it easy to enter.

4. Test and measure prizes and follow-up offers.

Rating: 4/5

Host Beneficiary

This is where you ask to promote yourself directly to the customers of another business. There are many ways to set it up. You could either offer the customers a gift voucher (and say that it is from the other business owner), offer to pay for the business owner's mailout, offer the business owner commission on any sales, or simply offer the favor in reverse. This can work exceptionally well for almost any type of business, and is especially good when you are friends with other businesspeople who have customers who fall into your target market.

Hints and Tips:

1. Ensure that the other businesses's customers are a *fit* with yours.

2. Make sure the company is reliable and has a good reputation.

3. Have a great headline and use *selling* words.

4. Think of an offer that combines both businesses.

5. Include a call to action.

6. Get the other business to endorse it.

7. Test and measure.

Rating: 5/5 +++

Strategic Alliances

This is where you join forces with other businesses and help each other. You could either market yourselves under the one name, making your joint business a *one-stop shop*, or just have a gentlemen's agreement to share customers, and refer them. These alliances really can pay off, especially if you find it difficult to get to your potential customers.

Hints and Tips:

1. There must be great synergy, both on a professional and personal level.

2. It must be a win/win situation.

3. Don't be afraid to ask—your best ally could be a former competitor.

4. Test and measure.

Rating: 5/5

Write a Book

This is an instant way to develop credibility, and actually have fun too. You can then market yourself as an expert, and even give the book away for free in order to get leads. Of course, it needn't be a full book—a small 10-page booklet could be enough.

Hints and Tips:

1. Come up with a catchy title and then work backwards.

2. Look to get it sponsored by a big business that might buy it in bulk and then mail it to their customers.

3. Send it to old and new prospects as a way of boosting your credibility.

4. Write it like you would talk it—that way it's much easier to read.

5. Have a picture of yourself on the cover.

6. Test and measure.

Rating: 3/5

Seminars and Events

Holding free or paid seminars is a great way to get your prospects in the same room all at once. Of course, this suits only a small percentage of businesses, mainly those with an informational product or service. Advertise the seminar, then follow up with the attendees.

Hints and Tips:

1. Have good speakers who are interesting.

2. Ensure that the venue is central and has ample parking.

3. Check what time your target market prefers—some groups prefer breakfasts while others an evening seminar.

4. Don't just do a "sell job." You must give people some useful information.

5. When marketing the seminar it's vital to have a terrific flyer with a really catchy headline that gets people's attention.

6. Test and measure.

Rating: 4/5

Trade Shows

Can work well if you select the right shows to participate in. Think carefully about the cost, and about how much you need to sell to make that money back. Will you make it back immediately, or in the very short term? Don't go just to *build awareness*—that's exactly the same as *wasting money*. When you display, make sure you do something different, and have something for people to look at. It's also important to get people's names and details, or better still, arrange to get the list of every person who attends.

Hints and Tips:

1. The people manning your stand must be knowledgeable and enthusiastic.

2. Have your product there so people can see it and maybe even try it.

3. Use the opportunity to research what your competitors are doing.

4. Have a special *show-only* offer.

5. Invest in some nice furniture to make the stand look professional.

6. Be proactive: Go out and grab people as they walk by. Use a powerful question and have something to show them.

7. Make sure the crowd is your target market.

8. Corner stands work best.

Rating: 4/5

Open Days and Sign-on Days

Can work for particular types of businesses. If you advertise it properly, and have enough incentives (goodies, entertainment, special deals), you're likely to get a decent turnout. These days can work as much for their entertainment value as anything else.

Hints and Tips:

1. Make it an *event* rather than just a sell job. Provide food, balloons, etc.

2. Test and measure.

Rating: 3/5

Party Plan

Selling your product via party plan takes a fair bit of organization but it can be worth it. This is where people (hosts) hold a party with their friends and demonstrate your product. Usually, you'll supply a demonstrator who will do the selling. The host receives a bonus if a certain amount of product is sold. This is ideal for products with appeal to middle-aged ladies. Investigate other party plan organizations before taking the plunge.

Hints and Tips:

1. Provide big incentives for your hosts to sell.

2. Spend the time creating a system that makes it as easy as possible for hosts to organize and execute the parties.

3. You'll need new and innovative products, so keep your eyes open.

4. Test and measure.

Rating: 4/5

Network Marketing

The "Amway" style of business. While many would consider networking out of favor, it is still a huge business—billions and billions are turned over every year. Does your product fit? To find out, ask yourself this question: "Is my product so good that anyone who uses it will literally beg their friends to buy it too?" To learn how to set it up, study the bigger networking companies.

Hints and Tips:

1. Go to some of the meetings network companies regularly put on.

2. There's much competition so the product needs to be a knockout to have any chance.

3. Your system of distribution and remuneration needs to be considered very carefully.

4. Ask yourself, "Am I the type of person that lends myself to multilevel marketing?"

5. Test and measure.

Rating: 2/5

Distributors or Agents

This is where you selectively allow your products or services to be sold or delivered through either individuals or other businesses. It can be a great way to quickly take your product national, or even international, but it all comes down to their reputation. If they do the wrong thing by customers when selling your product, then *you* look bad.

There are many different kinds of organizations that help match up suitable businesses. Check out your local chamber of commerce as a first stop. Of course, networking is also very effective.

As with any partnership it's very important to ensure that your goals and objectives are aligned, as well as your moral approach to business.

Hints and Tips:

1. Thoroughly check all applicants' reputations before agreeing to any deals. Ask for references so you can call and check their history.

2. Ensure that it's a win/win partnership.

3. Check that they don't distribute similar products you may be competing with.

4. Offer plenty of incentives to fuel motivation.

5. Make sure goals are aligned.

6. Test and measure.

Rating: 4/5

Licensees or Franchisees

Franchising has the potential to really kick-start a business. However, only a company with great systems can hope to succeed.

Take McDonald's, for instance. Ask people in a room to put up their hands if they think McDonald's make the best hamburger in the world and few will budge an inch. Then ask which hamburger business they would like to own and, you guessed it, they all choose The Golden Arches. Simple reason: It has a superb system that allows the business to run smoothly in the hands of 16-year-olds.

Even if you have a really good product and a great system that empowers any competent person to run a franchise successfully, you also need to consider current laws that may make it more complex and expensive than you thought to take this route. Designed to protect franchisees, it puts a huge up-front administrative burden on franchisors to prove the validity of their enterprise.

That said, it's definitely worth some thought.

Hints and Tips:

1. Don't skimp on your system; it must be outstanding.

2. Choose franchisees very carefully, as they are your representatives.

3. Don't go for franchisees just because they have money. Passion and determination are more important.

4. Check out the relevant legislation.

5. Test and measure.

Rating: 4/5

Market Days

Markets can work for certain types of products, but not all. It's important to bear in mind that people who come to markets are looking to buy, but only if it's cheap, a real bargain, or something completely out of the ordinary. If your product fits into one of those categories, it could be a good option. Remember: Most markets are "home-spun," meaning overt commercialization will be frowned upon.

Hints and Tips:

1. Choose carefully, as some markets will be a waste of time.

2. Don't commit yourself up front. Spend one weekend and then go from there.

3. Market shoppers are price conscious. so offer plenty of bargains and be prepared to haggle.

4. Try and offer products that are completely different.

5. Test and measure.

Rating: 4/5

Location

Sometimes your location can really get in the way. It may be worth changing location altogether, or perhaps opening other locations. When choosing a location, ask yourself the question, "How much new business will I get from being here?" Then "Considering that, is the rent reasonable?" Look for other factors, like trees that obscure your signage, or bad neighboring businesses that bring an unfavorable element in (unless that's who you're after). Remember, a better location is not the answer to everything, but it sure can help.

Hints and Tips:

1. If you're in retail, check for plenty of passing traffic.

2. Make sure that there aren't competitors right next door.

3. Don't sign a lease that locks you in for too long, although it's also nice to have secure tenure if the location is great. You need to weigh it up.

4. Ensure that the business name can clearly be seen.

5. Lots of parking is a big plus.

Rating: 4/5

Trade Longer or Different Hours

If you want to get the jump on your competitors, open at a different time, or for longer hours than they do. In some cases, it won't do a thing. For example, people are unlikely to want to come clothes shopping at 1:00 a.m. In the case of a hairdresser, though, people would love a salon that was open late every night of the week. How does it relate to you?

Hints and Tips:

1. Simply try it and see what happens.

2. Advertise it clearly—use it to help set you apart from the rest.

3. If it doesn't work, make sure people are given plenty of notice so they don't show up and get disappointed.

4. Test and measure.

Rating: 3/5

Referrals

One of the most powerful lead generators in the world. People spreading the word is a cheap and very effective means of lead generation. Obviously, this is achieved by offering exceptional value and service, but it can be further promoted by using special referral programs.

For example, you may reward people who introduce their friends with a free week's membership, or it could even be a *spotters* fee paid in the form of a gift voucher.

The key is not taking referrals for granted but rewarding those who are your best ambassadors.

Hints and Tips:

1. Offer a scheme where people know what they get for a referral.

2. Be very generous with those who spread the word. Think of what you would have to spend on advertising to get the same results.

3. Talk to other businesses that complement yours. You may be able to do a little reciprocal referring.

4. Test and measure.

Rating: 5/5

Test and Measure

It's strange, but just testing and measuring can help increase your number of leads. Knowing where your customers come from gives you the power to make smart decisions about what to spend your marketing money on.

Hints and Tips:

1. Keep meticulous records of where all leads are derived from and how much they spend.

2. Monitor how well every single product sells, and *why* it's selling.

3. Keep running marketing that works, even if *you* get bored doing it.

Rating: 5/5

YOUR FIVE KILLER LEAD GENERATION STRATEGIES

Now that you've read through this extensive list of proven lead generation ideas, and considered them in relation to your own individual situation, it's time to identify the five killer lead generation strategies most suited to your business.

Select the five you'd like to run with first and write the names of the strategies down on the form that follows. Next to each strategy fill in the date by which each is to be implemented.

This page, together with those for the next four parts of the Business Chassis, will form the basis of your instant marketing plan. They are your 25 killer marketing strategies.

LEAD GENERATION

Strategy 1: _____ Date: _____

Notes: _____
_____
_____
_____

Strategy 2: _____ Date: _____

Notes: _____
_____
_____
_____

Strategy 3: _____ Date: _____

Notes: _____
_____
_____
_____

Strategy 4: _____ Date: _____

Notes: _____
_____
_____
_____

Strategy 5: _____ Date: _____

Notes: _____
_____
_____
_____

Conversion Rate

This is where it all starts to happen. Once you get people through the door you must make the most out of every opportunity. You must turn those prospects into sales.

Conversion rates are often given little thought by the average business owners, and invariably when I ask them out of the blue, they take a guess. That's not good enough. You have to start measuring it *now*.

Regularly, business owners greatly overestimate the percentages. I remember one who guessed that she sold to "80 or 85 percent of people" who called or came into her business. After some serious testing and measuring we discovered it was nearer 35 percent. This came as a huge shock to the owner, but it also represents a tremendous opportunity.

Think of the bottom-line difference you can make by significantly boosting your conversion rate. If you can take your conversion rate from 30 percent to 60 percent, BAM, you've just doubled turnover.

So, do you know what your conversion rate is right now? If you don't, now's the time to quickly work it out. Here's how:

CONVERSION RATE

Start date: _____

End date: _____

Leads survey date: _____

Number of leads: _____

Number of sales transactions: _____

Conversion rate (transactions / leads x 100): _____

We're now going to work on the next part of your instant marketing plan, the section that aims to put strategies in place to dramatically improve your conversion rate.

It's possible, and here are the ways to make it happen.

58 WAYS TO BOOST YOUR CONVERSION RATE
Written Guarantee

This is where you write a guarantee addressing the customer's key frustrations in buying from you. For example, a hairdresser that guarantees "you will like your haircut and so will 98% of your friends." Or, what about the dentist who guarantees you "no pain?" Pick out the one thing that people are scared of when buying from you, and guarantee that it won't be a problem. If it is, offer to refund their money, or put things right. Once you've finalized it, make sure you tell people, and advertise it.

Hints and Tips:

1. Find out what your customers want above all else, and then promise to deliver just that.

2. The best way to find this out is by listening to your customers—they'll tell you.

3. Include this promise in all your literature and advertising. Make it a real selling point.

4. If you don't deliver on the promise, make sure your team is empowered to correct it or offer a refund.

5. Don't ever promise more than you can deliver.

Rating: 5/5

Define Your Uniqueness

If there's nothing different about you, people will only buy from you because of convenience or price, nothing more. Added to that, you'll never be able to raise your prices; if there's anyone doing it cheaper, people will buy from that business. You need to work out what is special about you, and then make a big deal about it. And don't just say *price* or *quality*. These are empty terms. Make it very specific, and meaningful.

Hints and Tips:

1. Sit down and ask yourself, "what is it that makes us stand apart from the rest?"

2. Once you know what sets you apart, tell the world, and tell it loudly.

3. Don't underestimate the power of uniqueness—simply by doing something different you can get lots of attention.

4. If there's nothing unique about what you do, start changing or adding things.

Rating: 5/5

Sell Your Own Product Line or an Exclusive Line

If you have something nobody else has, such as your own product line, people will be forced to buy it from you. Of course, you must make sure your products are up to scratch, and genuinely attractive.

Hints and Tips:

1. Develop or find something no one else has.

2. Look at what you are already doing—you may have something unique and you don't even know it.

3. If you haven't gotten anything exclusive yourself, develop partnerships that allow you to offer something special.

Rating: 3/5

Increase Range or Variety

The more you have, the more options you can give the customer, and the more individual tastes you can cater to. Naturally, you have to be careful you don't end up buying a bunch of highly specialized stock that you can never sell. In many cases, though, going from "Would you like an apple or an orange?" to "Would you like an apple, orange, or a banana?" can make a big difference.

Hints and Tips:

1. Look to diversify your range of products.

2. Keep your eyes open for items that complement what you currently offer.

3. Always try to offer more options to potential customers.

Rating: 3/5

Provide Quality Products

People will buy quality when it's affordable. By providing the best, you put yourself a cut above everyone else. And don't be afraid to mark up your products. People expect to pay more for quality, and they tend to regard higher-priced items as being of a higher standard.

Hints and Tips:

1. People will pay for quality, so don't be afraid to charge.

2. Have rigorous control checks because once a bad product hits the market the damage is done. Reputation is everything.

3. Scream the benefits and quality of the product. Leave no one in any doubt that this is a premium item.

4. Take nothing for granted. If you are offering a premium product, customers also expect premium service.

5. Sell up to quality, not down to price.

Rating: 4/5

Print a Benefits and Testimonials List

This is a sheet that you can give to people who come to look. It contains the four most important things about your product, or the seven reasons yours is a better choice for them. Make sure you use it each time. Alternately, print testimonials on it, that is, direct quotes from your past customers about how good you are. A mix of both can work very well.

Hints and Tips:

1. Help people make a decision by clearly explaining how it will positively benefit them.

2. Use testimonials to show customers that they weren't the first to buy this product—that it's OK to say *yes*.

3. Testimonials help reassure people's decisions—a real human need.

Rating: 5/5

Demonstrations

If you can demonstrate the product firsthand, do it. People like to see with their own eyes, and experience the product before they buy. If you can't demonstrate, think of a way you can do something similar—what about before and after photos? Or what about samples to give to the person to try? Taste tests are another option. Who hasn't gone for the dessert after having a sample?

Hints and Tips:

1. Make it real by showing how it works, tastes, feels, sounds, smells.

2. A demonstration is a great way to swing someone on the edge of a decision—all that's left is to see it in action!

3. Use videos for products that can't be demonstrated firsthand.

Rating: 5/5

Quality Brochures

Having a well-produced, full-color, glossy brochure can work wonders. It gives you the aura of professionalism and lets people really take their time to look over your offering in detail.

Hints and Tips:

1. Spend the time and money necessary to make it look professional. A bad brochure does more harm than having none at all.

2. Use plain English and lots of colorful pictures and diagrams.

3. Don't give too much information; this will just confuse.

Rating: 4/5

Offers

To seal the deal, throw in something they didn't expect, something that gives them the perception that they are getting a great deal. Then place a time limit on it, which pressures them into making a decision. Make sure it's something that they will value highly and which doesn't cost you very much. I know of a car lot, for instance, that offers buyers a "full tank of gas" if they sign today. You'd be amazed how many people are swung to buying a $50,000 car because of $30 worth of free gas.

Hints and Tips:

1. Look for low-cost products that have a high *perception* value.

2. Stipulate a time frame during which the offer is available.

3. Make the *special something* either useful or very memorable.

Rating: 5/5

Packaging

The more attractive the product looks, the better chance there is of selling it. Try redoing the packaging to make it look more modern, or perhaps even more traditional depending on what you are trying to achieve. Include benefits and features on the side of the package as well. It may also be an idea to package in value-added products—smaller accessories which may also serve as a lead into another product line.

Hints and Tips:

1. The packaging should represent the product.

2. The main aim is to grab people's attention.

3. Include *selling* words that people can relate to. Think of it as a small billboard.

Rating: 3/5

Display Awards and Certificates

The funny thing about certificates and awards is that it doesn't matter what they are, or what they were for. When people see framed awards or certificates, they think, "This place must be good." Even team awards will give the impression of quality. The only really relevant detail is the year. Displaying something with 1979 showing prominently may damage your chances of making the sale.

Hints and Tips:

1. Display everything you have won or been awarded (remembering to check the date).

2. Talk about accolades with customers.

3. Enter as many awards as possible—you may be surprised at the result.

Rating: 4/5

On-Hold Messages

Putting people on hold can either annoy the heck out of them, or encourage them to buy. If you have to put people on hold, why not take the opportunity of telling them all about your business at the same time: Why it's so good, what you sell, and why they should buy *today*.

Hints and Tips:

1. Use the tape not only to inform but also to *sell*.

2. Constantly update it, including time-sensitive special offers. This will make you look proactive.

3. Make it conversational and easy to understand.

4. Where possible, include testimonials read by some of your best customers.

Rating: 3/5

Account Applications

When people are buying, offering them an account can seal the deal. Offer to run through the application procedure on the spot. If they succeed (which they probably will), it's then as simple as saying "OK, I'll just put that on your account."

Making it as easy as possible for people to pay is one key to increasing your conversion rate.

Hints and Tips:

1. Do the procedure on the spot so they feel valued.

2. See if you can get a reference from one or more of their other creditors.

3. Keep meticulous records of all your debtors so it doesn't become an administrative nightmare.

Rating: 3/5

Mail Order

Allowing people to order from home can give you the edge. If you can take the hassle out of the buying procedure by letting them call and order, many customers won't balk at a higher price.

In this day and age of *time-starved* professionals, the convenience of home delivery is a real bonus.

Hints and Tips:

1. Do the costing carefully and ensure that you pass on the extra overhead to customers. People won't mind.

2. Tell the world: Mail order is a real selling point.

3. Throw something special into your mail order bag so when customers get their parcel, they also get a little surprise. And it doesn't have to be expensive to make an impact.

Rating: 4/5

Point-of-Sale Displays

What you do inside your shop is just as important as what you do outside. You have to advertise your products just as hard. Work on your displays, making them attractive, and if possible, interactive. Make tester bottles, or listening stations, or taste samples, always available. If people can experience the product without fear of being pressured, they will, and if they like it, they'll buy.

Hints and Tips:

1. Make them bright and colorful to attract attention.

2. Use *selling* words that convey the benefits.

3. If possible, have a sampler people can try.

Rating: 4/5

Use Payment Plans and Financing

This can get you over one of the biggest and most common hurdles: the price objection. If anyone says, "Can't afford it," you can say "But there is a way." Most customers love credit. It allows them to have things they can't really afford. Thankfully, most don't consider that it all catches up in the end.

Hints and Tips:

1. Wait till there's a price objection, then use your payment plan option.

2. Break down the total into palatable chunks: "That's only $75 a month."

3. Make sure they have the ability to pay back if you're burdened with the debt (no problem with credit cards).

Rating: 4/5

Take Credit Cards, Debit Cards, and Checks

There's no good reason not to. If people want to give you money, take it in whatever form they offer it. There are setup costs, but most businesses find the investment is worth it. There are now agencies that can help you "check on checks." You simply dial a number and find out if there's enough money in the account. No more bounced checks, and no more reason to not take them.

Hints and Tips:

1. People expect different methods of payment, so offer them!

2. Have all options available so there are no lame objections like, "I'll only buy from places where I can get Bonus Points."

3. Use credit checking and clearance companies to check on the larger amounts before you proceed with the sale.

Rating: 5/5

Audio and Video Sales Demonstrations

Why do all the hard work yourself? Instead, put your best sales spiel on tape (audio or video) and let it run continuously. People will stop and look, or tune in and listen. You can also send these tapes in the mail before an appointment, or follow up on the phone and sell directly. That's cheaper than a mobile sales rep!

Hints and Tips:

1. Invest in a quality recording or videotape. Remember that *you* are on show.

2. Keep it simple and focus on the benefits of the product.

3. Send it out before an appointment so there's already a sense of familiarity.

Rating: 5/5

Reprint Press Articles

If you've had anything printed about you (well, anything positive, that is), photocopy it and hand it to potential customers. This shows that other people know about you, and that you have a degree of *celebrity*. As weird as it may seem, people are attracted to this *star power*. It also builds credibility, because it seems as though someone objective is saying something nice about you.

Hints and Tips:

1. It gives instant credibility so use it as a sales tool.

2. Try and make color copies if possible.

3. Hang positive articles on your wall so all can see them.

Rating: 5/5

Rewrite Your Quotes, Tenders, and Proposals into Action Plans

Instead of just writing a standard quote (you get X for $Y—take it or leave it), why not write the prospect a letter? Include the price near the top, and then explain everything that makes you different. There's more to their decision than price, so make your letter, or plan of action, reflect that. End with, "I'll call in the next few days to discuss this further."

Hints and Tips:

1. Don't just focus on price. Also explain what makes you different.

2. Include a few testimonials.

3. Offer to "discuss it further" if there are any questions.

4. Keep selling *your promise*. It's the thing this client will want more than anything else.

5. Read Paul Dunn and Allan Pease's book, *Write Language.*

Rating: 5/5

Print Your Company's Vision Statement

Write out why you are in business, and your own personal standards. Include a summary of your ethics, and an outline of how you deal with customers. Then give it to every prospect—it will blow them away. Even better, get a calligrapher to do it up in nice writing, and print onto special paper.

Hints and Tips:

1. Have it professionally written up.

2. Be proud of it—give it out freely.

3. Spend some time on the words so each one is a winner. It should be very positive and inspiring.

Rating: 4/5

Use Prospect Questionnaires

Instead of going through the normal sale process, why not give prospects a questionnaire? Make it short, and wait with them while they fill it out, or better still, fill it out for them. Then, make your proposal fit their needs exactly. If they don't want to spend what you quote, suggest that you could do it for the price they want, but they may need to sacrifice a few things.

Hints and Tips:

1. Ask customers, "What exactly do you want?"

2. Compose a questionnaire with simple questions for them to complete.

3. Try to attach a value to everything they may want. This way they control the final price and they will know exactly what needs to be sacrificed if they want to stay under a certain figure.

Rating: 5/5

High Dress Standards and Uniforms

People base much of their decision on your appearance. If you look sleazy, customers will expect you to be a rip-off merchant. If you look professional, they will prefer to deal with you. Uniforms are ideal, as they add credibility and the feeling that the customer is dealing with a well-established, big organization. Name tags also work well, and allow the customers to feel they know you.

Hints and Tips:

1. Research colors and styles and ensure that your selection not only looks good but matches the image you're trying to project. For example, a funeral home uniform should look different from that of a vacation resort.

2. Try asking the customers what they would like to see you wear.

3. Also ask your team members. If they don't feel comfortable, they won't look comfortable.

Rating: 4/5

Try before You Buy

If you can do this safely, do it. It's the old "puppy dog" technique—try taking a puppy home then returning it two weeks later. Obviously, people won't have that kind of attachment to the product (unless you sell pets), but the product will become part of their lives. It will be twice as easy to say, "Which credit card would you like to pay for that on?"

Hints and Tips:

1. Make sure the prospective customer is genuinely interested in buying.

2. Ensure that they know exactly how the product works so they gain the maximum benefit from it over the trial period.

3. If you are out of demo products, offer to take their names and put them on a waiting list.

Rating: 4/5

Sales Scripts

Absolutely essential whatever business you're in. Once you find the right (or very close to right) way to sell something to someone, why change it? Write down exactly what you said, and then do that every time. And make sure your team does the same. Every customer is different, but the objective is always the same: Match the product to the buyer. You should have scripts for everything—from answering the phone to saying good-bye.

Hints and Tips:

1. Have a script prepared for every situation.

2. Make sure every team member has a copy.

3. Write the scripts in such a way they are easy to *talk*—nothing sounds sillier than a string of long words. Use questions most of all.

4. Test, measure, and be prepared to change any scripts with a lackluster performance.

Rating: 5/5

Build Trust and Rapport

There are some simple things that you can do to make sure this happens. First, always use their names, and make sure you introduce yourself using your full name. Ask them questions, and genuinely listen to the response—these are your clues. Provide ideas and advice, and do your best to help them. If you believe in your product, you should know that one of the best ways to help them is to sell them something.

Hints and Tips:

1. Spend more time listening than talking.

2. Remember their first names and then use them during the conversation. Remember that nothing sounds better to people than the sound of their own names.

3. Do everything you can to understand their concerns and then develop ways *(preferably together)* to solve them.

Rating: 5/5

Educate on Value, Not Price

Remember that people want a good deal, not the cheapest. They will be happier spending the dollars to get something that does exactly what they want, rather than spending less on a product that only does half the job. Explain why some people charge less, and what the prospects will miss out on if they do it on the cheap.

Hints and Tips:

1. Emphasize *value*.

2. Explain why your product is more expensive.

3. Compare yourself to others on quality and service, and all of a sudden price becomes almost irrelevant.

Rating: 4/5

Increase Product Knowledge

It's important to know as much about your product as you can. The more confident you sound when talking about it, the more likely your prospects are to regard you as the expert. People like to buy from people who seem to know what they're talking about. It gives them a sense of security.

Hints and Tips:

1. Always know more than a customer would about your product.

2. Study what the competition is doing. A customer may well ask.

3. Ensure that all your team members are as well educated about your product(s) as you are.

Rating: 4/5

Up-Sell, Cross-Sell, and Down-Sell

If you're having trouble selling something to a prospect, why not shift the focus to a different model? If it's a lack of quality, sell them a higher-priced item. If it has a high price, show them something you have that's cheaper. Or shift the focus to a model of a different color or a different shape.

Hints and Tips:

1. If negotiations stall, offer options.

2. Don't be afraid to introduce a customer to your other products.

3. Even if you have a sale, try to tag on something else.

Rating: 5/5

Use NLP Techniques

NLP stands for Neuro-linguistic Programming and was developed by John Grinder and Richard Bandler. It's a big enough subject to cover several books on it's own. It's all about communication modalities and understanding how people think, make decisions, learn, and understand.

There are so many NLP skills you can use to build rapport with people. For example, by "matching and mirroring" *(that is, copying the body language of your prospect)*, you will be able to start building instant rapport. You will instantly seem more trustworthy and familiar. Also match and mirror the skills of your prospects' communication modalities, that is visual, auditory, or kinesthetic. These skills alone can win you the sale. There are plenty of good books you can read on the subject.

Hints and Tips:

1. Monitor and mirror the body language of your prospects.

2. Match their words and the tonality, pitch, pace, and volume of their speech.

3. Read as much as you can on the subject.

Rating: 5/5

Sell on Emotion and Dreams

People tend to make their decisions based on emotion, not logic. In fact, emotion represents 88 percent of most purchasing decisions. Don't be afraid to get emotional with them—not in a teary-eyed way, but just by tapping into what makes them want the item. What are they going to use it for? How are they going to feel when they hold it in their hands tonight? What will their wife/husband think?

Hints and Tips:

1. Emphasize how the product is going to change their lives.

2. Focus on the emotional benefits of the product.

3. Spell out the benefits. Don't trust people to make the conclusions for themselves.

4. Ask emotionally focused questions.

Rating: 4/5

Follow Up and Follow Up Again

Don't let anyone slip through your fingers. Follow up until the point when the customers are becoming audibly annoyed with you. At this point, you're probably damaging your chances more than helping them. Keep calling until they buy, or they buy somewhere else. Until then, they're still *hot* prospects.

Hints and Tips:

1. Don't get disheartened—a *no* now could mean a *yes* in a week.

2. Don't be afraid to call back, again and again. After all, you have a great product.

3. Even if they don't buy from you, try to find out why and continue to maintain the relationship so they buy from you next time.

4. Ask for referrals.

Rating: 5/5

Ask for the Sale

Don't be shy. If you've asked enough questions, you should have established that the person wants to buy what you sell. If that's the case, assume the sale. Ask them an assumptive question like, "Would you like to pay for that on your credit card, or with cash?"

Hints and Tips:

1. Don't be afraid—you deserve the sale.

2. By not being a little aggressive you risk letting a hot prospect go who might just be hopeless at making decisions.

3. *Read* the situation carefully and ask the big question when you know you've sold all the benefits.

4. Word the question carefully—you don't want to sound too cocky!

Rating: 5/5

800 Number and Reply-Paid Address

Make it simple for people to deal with you. A toll-free number and reply-paid address means the barriers to people buying are slightly lower. If your competitors are offering this kind of service, you must also.

Hints and Tips:

1. Print them on all your correspondence and stationery.

2. Include the 800 number in advertising and in the phone book.

3. If possible, print your reply-paid address on an envelope that makes it even easier for people to respond, especially if you are direct mailing.

Rating: 3/5

Entertain, Wine, and Dine

It's the classic way to encourage people to buy: Build a strong relationship with them. This is especially the case if it's a big, service-oriented deal. People buy as much on your personality as on the merits of your product or service. A little schmoozing can go a long, long way, especially when your product or service is top notch too.

Hints and Tips:

1. Ask the prospect, "Where would you like to go?"

2. Don't skimp on things like wine and dessert. If you do it, do it properly.

3. Don't spend too much time talking shop. This is about having a good time and building the relationship.

Rating: 2/5

Run Competitions

Run a competition where the prize is something that will be superattractive to your target market. You can arrange the prize at an excellent price, or perhaps even free, as the company supplying the prize will be getting advertising out of it as well. Of course, you can offer the prize yourself. For example, people could win the purchase free but the only way they can enter is if they buy *today*.

Hints and Tips:

1. Link entering the competition with a call to action.

2. Try to do a deal with another company so the prize is free.

3. Keep all the names and addresses. This forms a valuable database.

Rating: 4/5

Train Team in Sales

Your business will only ever be as good as your employees, and most importantly, your front line, the salespeople. Get them to watch videos, read books, and attend seminars. Don't be afraid to pay for all of this; it's an investment in your business.

Hints and Tips:

1. Think of training as an investment, not a cost.

2. Get the salespeople to brief you on what they learned. This way you know they paid attention.

3. Get training yourself so you know what the best seminars are.

Rating: 5/5

Provide Team Incentives

If you offer something truly good, your sales team will try harder. It doesn't even need to be a prize. It could just be that they get to go home three hours early. Or what about a six-pack of beer for the month's highest-selling salesperson? Make the incentive challenging to win, yet accessible to all salespeople. If you have one "top gun" who always wins, the others will gradually become disenchanted and won't try. You could have one prize for the best service, one for the best ethics, and so on.

Hints and Tips:

1. Make the prize really enjoyable. Start by asking what people would really like to win.

2. Have a big ceremony so the person feels really special.

3. Ensure that you heap vast amounts of personal praise on the winner, as this recognition can mean a lot more than the prize.

4. Make it very clear what people need to do to win.

Rating: 4/5

Survey

Ask your customers, and the people who don't become customers, why they made the decision they did. What made some buy, and what prevented the rest? The results will give you incredible power—you'll know what "turns your customers on."

Hints and Tips:

1. Keep it short and simple.

2. Offer some kind of incentive to answer the questions, maybe going into a prize draw, or a gift check towards their next purchase.

3. After a week or so, send these people a thank-you letter including a few testimonials and some of your specials. Who knows, you might get some of those who didn't buy to give you another try!

Rating: 4/5

Provide a First Buyer's Incentive

That is, give something extra if it's the first time people have dealt with you. Naturally, this offer ends in a couple of days, so they'd better hurry.

Hints and Tips:

1. Look for a low-cost product with high *perception* value.

2. Make it extremely time sensitive so they have to act now!

Rating: 3/5

Store or Office Appearance

Work on it, then work on it some more. If your store or office looks untidy, people will feel cheap buying from you, and no one wants to feel cheap. The cleaner and more modern the store or office is, the better. It *will* increase your sales and is a worthy investment.

Hints and Tips:

1. Make it someone's mission (if not your own) to keep the place spotless—it must not be left to chance.

2. Always have plenty of products neatly displayed, as people tend to believe that what they see is what's available.

Rating: 3/5

Accept Trade-ins

This gives you the edge. It means that people can kill two birds with the one stone. They can buy something new, and get rid of the old. It also means you can charge a premium price. You can sell the old model to your customers, or sell it to another business. Alternatively, you may want to break it apart for parts.

Hints and Tips:

1. It's a great selling point, so use it in all you advertising and literature.

2. Establish partnerships with wholesalers, secondhand stores, etc., so you can maximize the value of old trade-ins.

3. Don't be afraid to increase your prices—you are offering a premium service now.

Rating: 3/5

Bulk Buy Specials

Encourage people to buy in bulk from you, and offer a significant saving if they do so. This also *ties* the people up for some time. You've loaded them up with stock, so they will not go anywhere else. They will also get used to using your product or service.

Hints and Tips:

1. The bigger the order, the bigger the discount.

2. Keep in contact with the customers. Just because they don't call you doesn't mean they aren't still using your product—they just bought so much!

Rating: 3/5

Scarcity and Limits

Use the best motivators in the world: fear and pain. If you make people think they're going to miss out, there's a good chance it'll swing the sale your way. That's especially right if you also infer that you can't get any more. Beware, though, people know this trick, so be subtle.

Hints and Tips:

1. Use this tactic only if it seems genuine.

2. Make it quite clear that it's a case of first in, first served.

3. Imply that there's no guarantee when this product will again be made available.

Rating: 5/5

Change Your Direct Mail Pieces

You should be constantly improving you marketing material. Once it works, keep it, but occasionally try something different. Even the best pieces of direct mail can become stale at some point. Give it a rest, try something a little different, and then come back to it later.

Hints and Tips:

1. Keep it fresh and interesting.

2. Constantly monitor, review, and revise.

3. Observe what others are doing and borrow what works.

4. Test and measure

Rating: 4/5

Collect All Prospects' Details

This is essential. Ask all prospects who come in if they'd like to join your mailing list. Most will say yes and give you whatever details you ask. From then on, you can follow up.

Hints and Tips:

1. Ask all prospects for their addresses.

2. Ask in such a way that it seems like you are doing them a favor: "We need your address so we can send you all the latest designs as we get them."

3. Don't be too pushy. Some people are very reluctant to give out their details, and you don't want to jeopardize a sale over one address.

Rating: 5/5

Give Away to Get Back

If you start the relationship unselfishly, offering advice and assistance, you'll discover that you'll be ultimately rewarded with a sale. Never think you've wasted your time helping someone. In the long run it will pay off handsomely.

Hints and Tips:

1. Give advice freely without any connotation of obligation.

2. Think of it as a *long-term* investment.

Rating: 3/5

Factory or Site Tours

Inviting people to take a tour of your factory can really boost your credibility. If people see how things are made, and the craftsman at work, they are more likely to believe you when you talk about quality.

Hints and Tips:

1. Get your team involved so they are prepared for the tour.

2. Ensure that everything is spotless.

3. Really plan it well, explaining the history of your business and the most interesting things you do.

4. At the end of the tour, offer free samplings of what you produce.

Rating: 3/5

Target Better Prospects

If you're having serious trouble with your conversion rate, you may want to go back and have another look at the way you attract prospects. Are you getting the right sort of people? If not, how else could you advertise? It's important to remember that some prospects are more trouble than they are worth.

Hints and Tips:

1. Class your prospects into A, B, C, and D and treat them accordingly.

2. If you aren't getting enough As and Bs (these are the people who buy big and buy often), review your lead generation strategies.

3. Note that any customer isn't necessarily a good customer.

Rating: 4/5

Company Profile

This can work as a serious sales tool. You create a five- to six-page document detailing what makes your company so great. More importantly, talk about why your company is the best choice for the prospects, and what you plan to do for them.

Hints and Tips:

1. Don't be afraid to boast.

2. Include testimonials

3. Use *selling* words

4. Focus on how your company helps solve people's problems.

Rating: 4/5

Gimmicks with Direct Mail

Include something out of the ordinary: a tea bag, a lollipop, or something even more bizarre. This will ensure that your direct mail letter is remembered when you phone.

If possible, find out a bit of background information on your prospects, as this will help you choose something they will really find memorable.

Hints and Tips:

1. Make it different.

2. Personalize it if possible.

3. Try to tie it in with a big news story or something topical that's happening. This makes you look proactive.

Rating: 4/5

Charge for Normally Free Advice

This will set you up as the expert, and put you in a far better position when it comes to crunch time. You may not deal with as many prospects, but every one you do deal with will be well qualified.

Hints and Tips:

1. Put a price on your time and knowledge.

2. Use that credibility as leverage when it comes to making the sale.

Rating: 4/5

A Gift Check Towards Purchase

Include a gift check with your letter that people can spend on anything you have to offer. Works best when your product is midpriced, and the voucher accounts for about 10–15 percent of the purchase price. Make the voucher a dollar amount, not a percentage.

Hints and Tips:

1. Make sure it's time sensitive—"valid for this week only."

2. Include a couple *(so they can give one to a friend)*, but stipulate only one per person.

Rating: 5/5

Always Have Stock on Hand

That means you can say to people, "And of course, you can take this home today. I have one in stock." This makes it far more immediate for them. There's no bigger turnoff after getting excited by a product to then be told there's a two-week waiting list.

Hints and Tips:

1. Always have enough stock so people can take one home immediately.

2. If you are out of stock and the product allows, offer them a demo that will be replaced when new stock arrives.

Rating: 4/5

Offer Exclusivity

Letting people know that they have the opportunity to be your only client can make them feel excited. It can also have the impact of making them want to buy now to solidify the deal.

Hints and Tips:

1. If you can offer exclusivity, make sure you get a premium price for the prestige factor.

2. Ensure that you can keep the promise if you make it.

Rating: 5/5

Allow Prepayment

Allow people to pay before the goods have arrived. You may even want to offer a discount, or an added value product, to encourage this. The department stores use this technique very successfully by offering layaway as an option.

Hints and Tips:

1. Offer some kind of incentive; it helps with planning your inventory.

2. Make sure the offer features prominently in your advertising.

Rating: 4/5

Set Sales Targets

Give your salespeople a clear idea of what you need them to achieve. Explain the exact reasons why they need to achieve it, and outline your financial situation. Offer bonuses if they meet the targets. People want to succeed but can only do so if they know by what measure they will be judged.

Hints and Tips:

1. Set clear targets.

2. Explain why these targets need to be met.

3. Offer appealing bonuses for accomplishment.

4. Provide plenty of encouragement to those who beat the target.

Rating: 5/5 +++

Measure Conversion Rates

When you do, you'll find almost invariably that your conversion rate improves. Of course, you won't know for sure, because you've never measured it before, but you'll start to focus on selling to the people who come in the door.

If you have sales reps on the road, get them to fill out performance analysis sheets each day. Here's an example of what it might look like:

SALES PERFORMANCE

Rep: _____ Date: _____

Customer	Sale (Y/N)	Item Bought	$ Amount
_____	_____	_____	_____
_____	_____	_____	_____
_____	_____	_____	_____
_____	_____	_____	_____

If you employ telemarketers, you also need to measure their performance. Get them to fill in a sheet similar to the example below. It records whether their call is incoming or outgoing.

TELESALES PERFORMANCE				
Rep: _____ Date: _____				
CustomerSale	(Y/N)	Item Bought	$ Amount	Call (In/Out)
_____	____	_____	_____	_____
_____	____	_____	_____	_____
_____	____	_____	_____	_____
_____	____	_____	_____	_____

Hints and Tips:

1. Test and measure everything you do.

2. If it is not working, don't be afraid to change. After all, there are hundreds of ways to do that right here in this book.

Rating: 5/5 +++

YOUR FIVE KILLER CONVERSION RATE STRATEGIES

It's now time to consider the proven ideas of increasing your conversion rate and evaluating them in relation to your own particular situation. All may work for you, but which will you try first?

It's possible, of course, that you already use some of them, and if that's the case, great. They will already be working for you and accounting for your present conversion rate.

It's time now to put strategies in place to increase the conversion rate you currently enjoy. It's time to add to what you're already doing. You see, it's all about looking for ways to multiply for profits, not just add to them.

Identify the five killer conversion rate strategies you think are most suited to your business right now.

Select the five you'd like to run with first and write the names of the strategies down on the form that follows. Next to each strategy fill in the date by which each is to be implemented.

This page, together with that for the previous part of the Business Chassis as well as those for the next three, will form the basis of your *25 killer marketing strategies* and your *instant marketing plan*.

CONVERSION RATE

Strategy 1: _____ Date: _____

Notes: _____

_____

_____

_____

_____

Strategy 2: _____ Date: _____

Notes: _____

_____

_____

_____

_____

Strategy 3: _____ Date: _____

Notes: _____

_____

_____

_____

_____

Strategy 4: _____ Date: _____

Notes: _____

_____

_____

_____

_____

Strategy 5: _____ Date: _____

Notes: _____

_____

_____

_____

_____

Number of Transactions

Once you've made a sale, you need to make another, and another, and another—to the same person.

You should know the statistics: It costs six to seven times more to get a new customer than it does selling to an old one. It's no news flash, but it's true!

People that do business with you represent a gold mine of opportunity. You must collect their details, get to know them, treat them as special, keep in constant contact, and regularly invite them back as members of the family. These people are either going to make you rich or make you poor.

But before we start looking at ways of getting rich, do you know how many times your customers buy from you at present?

We're talking averages here, not the best or worst case. If you don't, then find out now. You see, if you don't know what your average number of transactions is, how will you be able to gauge whether you've been able to increase it through the strategies you're about to put in place? And how will you know which of them are working and which aren't?

Here are a few ideas on how to go about measuring your current number of transactions:

1. If you have customer accounts, select a representative sample. Choosing 50 at random will do. Or choose all those whose surnames start with *M*. Then make a list of the number of times each purchased from you over the last 12 months. The list will have wide variances, because some might have bought once while others might have bought 20 times. That's OK. Add up the number of times they all purchased. This will give you a total of the number of transactions they all made over the period. Now divide this total by the number of customers. You'll now have the average number of transactions.

2. If you don't have customer accounts, you could survey your customers. Use a form similar to this:

NUMBER OF TRANSACTIONS SURVEY

Start Date: _____

End Date: _____

Survey Date: _____

Customer Name: _____

Address: _____

Number of Transactions: _____

---

3. If you have a database containing customer details and the transactions they make, use this to calculate an average.

4. If you don't have access to any of the above, then estimate a figure. Give it your best shot. Try watching customer activity in your business over the next few days to see if you can detect a pattern. Factor in the type of stock you sell—is it fast-moving consumables or expensive, slow-moving goods? Do you recognize some of your clientele by sight or do you know them by name? Do you recognize many of them or just a few? Ask them how many times they deal with you on average. They'll tell you. Then factor in those you don't know. How many do you think buy only once? How many are occasional shoppers? The vast majority? This could sway your result downwards.

Of course, the time frame you use is very much dependent on the type of business you run. If you sell cars, your average customer might buy only once or twice every three years or so, but if you run a fast-food outlet, the averages would be very much higher. In this case you could take a snapshot over a three-week period and extrapolate the result for an annual figure.

Let's look at some ways of getting rich.

50 STRATEGIES FOR BOOSTING YOUR NUMBER OF TRANSACTIONS
Better Service to Make Your Customers Special

It seems obvious, but treating your customers in a special way can make a big difference. Spend a little extra time with them, and don't be afraid to develop a genuine bond with them—find out what their interests are, where they live, what they think. And always go that extra mile, as this makes the customer really remember you.

Hints and Tips:

1. Get to know your customers' interests.

2. Use the customer's first name as much as possible.

3. Find out if they are married and what their kids' names are; then do something for the family if possible. This is very powerful.

4. Don't take anyone for granted. Constantly ask, "Is there anything we could do better?"

Rating: 4/5

Underpromise and Overdeliver

Although it sounds simple, underpromising is tricky. It means not tooting your own horn and only giving away enough bait to hook the customers. That means you need something in reserve. If you tell them it will be in stock on Wednesday, get it in on Tuesday, and call them on Monday afternoon to let them know. Always try and do a little more than they expect. If you just do what you promise, you'll probably get them back next time. If you do what you promise plus a whole lot more that they weren't expecting, you'll have customers for life. It's worth it.

Hints and Tips:

1. Actually *do* more than you promise.

2. Keep something special up your sleeve so you can surprise them.

3. Remember, it's the small things that can make a big difference.

Rating: 5/5

Deliver Consistently and Reliably

One bad experience can *kill* good customers. It's true. Even if you've built up a good relationship, treating them badly one time can make them think about going somewhere else. It's funny, but the better your service is, the more they expect, and the more disappointed they'll be if you let them down. The most important thing is not to get complacent. You need to be consistent and reliable. Whether they are new or old customers, give them your best.

Hints and Tips:

1. Regardless of the how long you've been dealing with people, treat them well every time.

2. The more good service people get, the more they expect.

3. Remember, you're only as good as your last encounter.

Rating: 5/5

Keep in Regular Contact

You should be in contact at least once every three months. Ideally, mail something to your customers every three months, even if it's just a postcard or e-mail with a funny message. A phone call to make a special offer is also an excellent idea. Remember, your business is probably one of the lowest priorities in your customers' lives—they *will* forget about you if you don't keep in contact.

Hints and Tips:

1. Keep in contact every six weeks or at least quarterly.

2. Make your correspondence memorable.

3. Include special offers.

Rating: 5/5

Inform Customers of Your Entire Range

Often, people only know part of your range. If you introduce them to another part, the results can be huge. You'll be surprised how many customer say, "Oh, you mean I can buy my [x] here too?" or "Yeah, I wouldn't mind trying that." They already trust you and your main product. Now introduce them to the rest of your products/services. Far too many business owners assume their customers know about everything they sell.

Hints and Tips:

1. Once you have their trust, use it to introduce them to new products.

2. The more products they buy from you, the more likely they are to keep coming back.

Rating: 5/5

Increase Your Range

If you only have one product that people buy irregularly, or only once every few years, you need to expand your range. Sell accessories, or something related, yet quite different. You'll be surprised by how many people will buy from you, just because you treated them well last time. Write them a letter, or call them and let them know of your new product additions.

Hints and Tips:

1. Look for products that complement your existing range.

2. Inform all your old customers about these exciting new additions to your range.

3. Don't forget to keep reminding them about your original product(s) as well.

Rating: 4/5

Increase Product Obsolescence/Upgrades

That is, give your products a shorter life span, either by reducing their quality (a risky proposition), or by developing new models that customers simply *must* have. The fashion business would not survive without this technique. Every few months, we are encouraged to scrap our entire wardrobe and "get with the times." How can you apply this idea to your business? Perhaps you could improve your product and allow people to trade in the old model.

Hints and Tips:

1. Look for ways people can *enhance* a product they've already bought from you.

2. Always introduce *new and improved* versions.

3. Have a trade-in option.

Rating: 3/5

Always Have Stock

If you don't, you could easily lose customers. See, people like to be sure of two things when dealing with a business: one, that they're getting a reasonable deal and two, that they can rely on the business to help them. If you're out of stock most times they call, your customers will eventually start going somewhere else— somewhere with stock.

Hints and Tips:

1. Predict sudden rushes and stock up accordingly.

2. If finances are tight, see if you can get stock on consignment.

3. Make sure you deal with products you can readily get more of.

Rating: 4/5

Offer Service Contracts

Don't just sell to a customer once. Build in long-term sales with a service contract up front. Offer a five-year, a two-year, and a one-year contract. People will generally take the one-year contract.

And, if you're constantly servicing your customers' purchase, you'll know when it needs replacing. You'll also have the direct opportunity to sell them accessories, or get referrals. Make the service contracts very attractively priced—it's as much an investment in your future earnings as it is a service.

Hints and Tips:

1. Get a commitment from people to bring the product back to you for service. This can be done by offering incentives or voiding warranty claims if they take it elsewhere.

2. When they come for the service, use it as an opportunity to sell them other products.

Rating: 4/5

Keep Clients' Vital Information

This is the best way to tie up a client forever. If you want an example, think about doctors. Why do people go to the same doctor every time? First, because of trust. But more importantly, the doctor has your files, your whole medical history. How can you apply the idea? Mechanics, hairdressers, plumbers, beauty therapists, and natural healers can all do it very simply. Just make sure your customers know that they now have a file with you.

Hints and Tips:

1. Take the time to get as much information as possible on the first visit.

2. Use the file every time your customers come into contact with you so they start appreciating its value.

3. Review and update the file at every visit.

Rating: 5/5

Product of the Week

Featuring products and offering good deals on them is an excellent way to get people to branch out. People love a bargain—if you let them know that there will be one every week, they'll keep their eyes peeled, and jump on anything that excites them. Beyond that, it has the effect of making them want to stay in contact.

Hints and Tips:

1. Always have at least one great deal that attracts customers.

2. Introduce a new special every week or month so people start looking forward to it.

Rating: 3/5

Ask Them to Come Back

Sounds silly, right? Wrong. It's something most businesses overlook. How many hairdressers ask to book you for your next appointment at the end of the first one? Some do, but they often word it wrongly. You see, they expect that people don't want to plan that far ahead. It depends on how you ask. Try saying something like this: "Have you been happy with our session today? Great. I'd like to book you for your next session now. That should ideally be in six weeks. I could fit you in on Thursday night, or Saturday morning. I'm pretty heavily booked already. Which of those times suit you best?" If they say *no*, ask them if you can call and remind them in six weeks.

Hints and Tips:

1. Ask before they leave, "Shall we make an appointment for next time, or should I call you in a few weeks to make the booking?"

2. Make the sale, but remember to word it carefully so people don't feel you're being too pushy.

3. Make it sound as though you are doing them a favor.

Rating: 5/5

Send Out a Newsletter

Absolutely essential for businesses where people only buy once every few months or more. You must keep in regular contact, and a newsletter is an ideal way. Not only can you advertise any product you want, you can also include tips, articles, and more. Some businesspeople even include extracts of their own poetry (not always advisable!). If you include enough good information, people will read, and more importantly, they will buy.

Hints and Tips:

1. Make practical information the number-one priority of the newsletter.

2. Keep the stories brief and written in plain English.

3. Use as many pictures and graphics as possible.

4. Subtly include products and specials with calls to action.

5. Make sure the newsletter comes out at regular intervals so people start expecting it.

Rating: 4/5

Run a Frequent Buyers Program or VIP Card

The classic method of getting customers to come back. Give them a card that gets stamped every time they buy. You may want to offer every sixth purchase free, or a special gift on the tenth purchase. Work out the number and what you can afford, but make it generous. If it's a poor and pathetic offer, people will be completely disinterested.

Hints and Tips:

1. Have a great offer that isn't easily forgotten.

2. Keep reminding people how close they are getting to the goal.

3. Make it easy to keep track of customers' progress, as they may well lose the card. If possible you should keep all the records yourself.

Rating: 5/5

Collect a Database

This should be something you are already doing. If it isn't, you *must*. There isn't really a business on the planet that proves an exception to the rule—collect names at all costs. All you need to do is say, "I'd like to add you to my mailing list. Can you fill this out please?" Alternately, you could just say, "We regularly mail out specials to our customers. Just fill this out and you'll be the first to know." You can also run a competition, or just go through your invoices.

Hints and Tips:

1. Always ask for your customers' details—*no* exceptions.

2. Offer an incentive and word the request in such a way that they feel they are benefiting from it.

3. If people won't give you their names, don't push it.

Rating: 5/5

Give Out Key Rings, etc.

This can work well if it's tied in with good service also. People won't give a hoot about your key ring if you've kept them waiting 20 minutes, then overcharged them for a botched job. If, on the other hand, the customers were impressed, the key ring may act as a handy reference when they want to call you again. Remember, the only people likely to get excited by a "Jim's Plumbing" key ring are Jim, his wife, and his mother. Think about a gift that will be useful and meaningful to your customers.

Hints and Tips:

1. Make the gift useful and, if possible, a little different.

2. Use *selling* words on the gift so people can quickly remember what it is you do three months down the track when they see it.

3. Clearly include all your contact details.

Rating: 3/5

Presell or Take Prepayments

Why not sell to people while they're in the mood, such as after you've served them in a truly impressive way? You could ask people for a deposit on their next purchase, and offer them an incentive to do so. Alternately, you could sell them a package deal.

Hints and Tips:

1. Always be ready to sell, even after you've just made a sale.

2. Offer incentives for people to do more business with you.

3. Bundle up your products and try and do a package deal.

Rating: 4/5

Contracts

This will work only in select industries, but it's certainly the most potent way to keep people coming back. Assuming you continue giving good service, your customers will never leave you.

Hints and Tips:

1. Ensure that it's a win/win situation so they spread the word about your business.

Rating: 4/5

Until Further Notice Deals

Can work extremely well, especially for consumable (and that doesn't just mean edible) products. The idea is that you continue to deliver the product *until further notice*. That is, until they tell you to buzz off. You have their credit card number, and just charge it each time you deliver. Obviously, there needs to be an incentive for the customer to agree—convenience is one, but something financial will also help.

Hints and Tips:

1. This is a big benefit to you so offer strong incentives.

2. Make sure they are clear on the arrangement so they don't dispute it after you've sent them several products.

3. No news is good news with this setup, but you still need to subtly monitor the customer's satisfaction.

4. At all times see if you can add to the products that are being sent *until further notice*.

Rating: 5/5

Plan Future Purchases

If you have a product that is being constantly updated, why not help your customers out and plan their future purchases with them? For example, a computer store could make a date to call them in 12 months to discuss an upgrade. A car dealer could let the customer know of the time line for releases of future models, and make a tentative rough time to call.

Hints and Tips:

1. Ask up front to arrange a follow-up call when it's time for an upgrade.

2. In the time between the call and follow-up, keep in contact so no one else invades your turf.

Rating: 4/5

Offer on Next Purchase

Can be risky, as the customer may come to expect something for nothing every time and you will end up never getting full price for your service. If you're having trouble bringing people back, though, it can be a good idea. Simply giving them a gift check to spend with you next time they come back can work wonders, as can a "Buy before this date and I'll give you this" deal.

Hints and Tips:

1. Make sure you can afford to make the offer.

2. It should only be used if stock is moving very slowly.

3. You don't need big gifts or discounts, just a little sweetener should do.

Rating: 4/5

Reminder System

Works brilliantly for mechanics, dentists, and other businesses that take care of the things that we tend to forget. For example, people will actually appreciate a note in the mail that says "Just a reminder—it's been four months since your last car service. You really should come back within two weeks. I'll call within two days to arrange a time." Florists can use the idea too. By getting a list of their customers' mothers' birthdays, their spouses' mothers' birthdays, and everyone in between, they can make lots more sales. Every time a special occasion occurs, they can call and say "I notice it's your mom's birthday. Would you like me to send her a $35 bouquet?"

Hints and Tips:

1. Compile a list of the special dates in a customer's life so you can send special reminder notices.

2. With the note should be a special offer including a call to action.

3. Try and somehow personalize each note.

4. You might include, "If I don't hear back from you, I'll call within the next two days." This way you hedge your bets.

Rating: 5/5

Accept Trade-ins

If your product is regularly updated and improved, it's worth accepting trade-ins on the old models. You can sell the secondhand models at a top margin and make a killing.

Hints and Tips:

1. Make sure you have avenues to sell or off-load the trade-ins.

2. Tell the world about it. This is probably a real point of difference from other businesses, unless you sell cars!

Rating: 3/5

Increase Credit Levels

If you trust your customers as good payers, why not send them a letter that says: "Because of your excellent payment record, your credit level has been increased." People, being the "live today, deal with the consequences tomorrow" creatures they are, will probably come in and buy up plenty more.

Hints and Tips:

1. Be confident about the customers' ability to repay.

2. When sending the letter, include some of the great products that are now within their reach.

3. Have a call to action or offer a special incentive to act quickly.

Rating: 3/5

Target Likely Repeaters

To ensure that you build a business based on repeat business, go after the right people in the first place. That is, the people who are likely to come back time and time again. Give it some thought. Who buys your product on a regular basis?

Hints and Tips:

1. Understand that some customers are *much* better than others.

2. Try and identify a pattern of repeat business customers and then target that group vigorously.

Rating: 4/5

Postpurchase Reassurance

A fancy name for helping people to feel OK about their decision to buy from you. You could send them press articles on the product, or recent favorable reviews. Even testimonials from your own customers could work well. Think of how good you feel when the shop assistant says, "Gee, that shirt looks great on you." Even though it's his job, you are still more likely to buy it. And because most people are born followers, constant reminders that they are doing the right thing by doing business with you is important.

Hints and Tips:

1. In subtle ways keep telling customers, "You did the right thing."

2. Constantly update them with favorable press coverage and any new information that shines a positive light on your product.

3. Use testimonials as often as possible.

4. A simple thank-you card is a great start.

Rating: 5/5

Suggest Alternative Uses

Why not mail your customers an information sheet detailing different ways to use your product, or alternatively, highlighting features they may have never used? This will add to their satisfaction and make them more likely to buy next time.

Hints and Tips:

1. Look for new and innovative ways to use your product.

2. Relay these thoughts through regular contact.

Rating: 3/5

Special Occasion Cards

You can build the relationship further by sending out cards on the customers' birthdays, and at Christmas. You could also send them a one-year anniversary card—that is, one year since they bought from you. If they are rabid golf fans, it could be a card reminding them not to miss a minute of the U.S. Masters that is being playing next week. The possibilities are limited only by your creativity and how much information you have gathered on the person.

Hints and Tips:

1. Keep detailed files on your customer so you know when important dates arise.

2. Don't underestimate the relationship-building power of a simple birthday card—very few businesses do it.

Rating: 4/5

Direct Mail Regular Offers

Practically every business should be doing this. You should mail your customers an outline of special offers. You can pick products or services that they have never tried, or offer package deals on something they have.

Hints and Tips:

1. Make it a regular practice to contact customers with new products or special offers.

2. Include a call to action.

3. Make it sound special: "Look what I've brought into stock just for you."

Rating: 4/5

Follow Up and Follow Up Again

It's important to be persistent—don't let your customers slip through your fingers. Follow up. If they don't respond, follow up again, but stop before you become annoying. If you don't, you could lose the customers forever.

Hints and Tips:

1. Don't get lazy; keep on their case.

2. Try to make every contact a little different.

3. Importantly, you need to know when to stop!

Rating: 5/5

Telemarket

Regularly phone your customers, and ask them to buy. You could do this under the guise of a quarterly satisfaction check, or to follow up recent direct mailings such as a newsletter. It's essential to have a powerful and natural sales script.

Hints and Tips:

1. Ensure that a great sales script, with lots of questions, is ready.

2. Have a good reason for making the call, then move in for the sale.

3. Offer a great deal on the main item you are trying to sell.

Rating: 4/5

Run Competitions

Mail to your customers, and again ask them to buy. If they do, you'll automatically put them into the drawing for something they'd dearly love to have. The trick to competitions is to make the prize something exciting and rare, and to make the people believe that there is a reasonable chance they may win.

Hints and Tips:

1. Offer a great prize.

2. Give the impression that the chances of winning are very good.

3. Include a call to action.

Rating: 3/5

Past Customer Events

Why not have a cocktail party and invite all your past customers? People are always looking for ways to meet other people, and may come along to your party for that alone. You don't need to pay for all the drinks, but it can help. Of course, it doesn't have to be party. You could send them tickets to a sporting event, or something similar.

Hints and Tips:

1. Promote it as a terrific networking opportunity.

2. Make people feel as though they are part of a select few who have been invited.

3. Check what time of day they would prefer and tailor it accordingly.

4. Offer a special gift to all those who attend.

5. Make it a really enjoyable occasion (not just another sales opportunity), or people will respond very negatively.

Rating: 4/5

Closed-Door Sales

Write to your customers and invite them to an exclusive sale where only past customers are invited, and the doors are locked to all other people. The sale occurs after hours, and the bargains are especially good. It pays to provide drinks and snacks—you'll find most people don't touch them anyway.

Hints and Tips:

1. Give it an air of exclusivity: something bound to get people interested.

2. Make sure the items for sale are really *special*.

3. Give them an extra invitation to bring along a friend.

Rating: 5/5

Fax Sales

Fax your past customers a list of specials, limited for 30 days. Emphasize that there is a limited number of each and that they must act now. These specials are only for past customers. An excellent way to clear stock and generate cashflow.

Hints and Tips:

1. Have a couple of really great deals.

2. Explain the benefits of the products, using *selling* words.

3. Keep the fax simple. A price list with discounts is best. Send it to them, but accept orders via fax only after a certain time on a certain day.

4. Use a really catchy headline.

5. Include a call to action.

Rating: 5/5

Named Promotional Gifts

This can be a good way to ensure that your customers hang onto your number. Give them something useful, and depending on your profit margins, make it something meaningful.

Hints and Tips:

1. Find a quality product that has durability.

2. Clearly detail what you do and where you can be contacted.

3. If the product can be personalized, so much the better.

Rating: 3/5

Information Nights

Why not invite your customers to an information night on a new product or service. You could suggest that they will be the first people to see a new model, or new innovation. Either aim for sales on that night, or follow up later.

Hints and Tips:

1. Make it sound exciting: "First time in this country."

2. Offer a gift or discount to those who attend.

3. Get people to fill out feedback forms.

4. Make the presentation interesting—you may need a speaker who can liven things up.

Rating: 3/5

Free Upgrades

Offer your customers free upgrades or another complimentary product if they buy a pack of accessories. Or, offer a guaranteed trade-in price whenever they are ready to move up to the next model. You'll see more sales, and you'll be guaranteed that the customer will return for the upgrade. Even better, use no-cost upgrades to reward your best customers.

Hints and Tips:

1. Offer specials to encourage people to buy in bulk or take package deals.

2. Think long term. It may be viable to sacrifice a little margin now in order to ensure the customer's return in the future.

Rating: 3/5

Socialize with Clients

Why not? Many of your clients are probably into the very same things that you are. It's likely you'll develop a strong bond with them. Just invite them out for dinner some time, or invite them to a big party at your place. People find it hard to change businesses after they've come to know the owner personally.

Hints and Tips:

1. Make friends with your customers.

2. Spend time with them away from the work environment.

3. Find out what they like to do and then organize such an activity.

4. Spend as much time as possible *listening*, as this will endear you to them.

5. Inviting them to your home can be a nice touch *(just make sure you do the cleaning beforehand)*.

Rating: 3/5

Labels and Stickers

Especially good when you service a particular piece of equipment, such as the customer's computer, hot water system, or car. Just put a sticker on it which says, "Problems? Call XXX-XXXX."

Hints and Tips:

1. In simple language, explain what you do, using *selling* words.

2. Make sure people feel they can call you anytime.

3. Use bright colors and easy-to-read fonts.

4. Include every possible way someone can contact you.

Rating: 5/5

Catalogs

Mail out catalogs to your customers, with an ordering page. This allows them to simply reorder without any inconvenience. It's a good idea to follow up on the phone.

Hints and Tips:

1. Include plenty of specials with bonuses for multiple purchases.

2. The order form should be easy to fill out.

3. All payment methods should be available.

4. Follow up with a phone call if people haven't responded.

5. Have special deals linked with a call to action.

Rating: 3/5

Cooperative Promotions

If you're stuck for ideas on how to boost your number of transactions, why not sell other people's product or service? Take a commission, just as if it were your own product. Many people don't even consider this option, but if their products don't compete with yours, chances are they'd be delighted to gain another distribution source.

Hints and Tips:

1. Look for products that have a synergy with yours.

2. Make sure you deal with a reputable company.

3. Continuously check the quality of the product.

4. Strike a deal that leaves plenty of incentive for both parties.

Rating: 5/5

Rent/Sell Your Database

Either sell it outright, or take a piece of every sale the person renting it makes. Make sure you investigate the business first—your customers may get irate if you give some shyster access to their details. If possible, check the offer before it gets sent out.

Hints and Tips:

1. Thoroughly check all companies who use your database.

2. Make sure they are offering a quality product that represents value.

3. Check what literature they are sending out. Does it look professional?

4. Don't overdo this strategy or you'll lose all credibility with customers.

Rating: 3/5

Clean Up Your Database

Every six months, call all the people on your database and check their details. You may be wasting thousands of dollars sending mail to people who have recently moved, or who are deceased.

Hints and Tips:

1. Use it as an opportunity to reestablish the relationship.

2. Have a great sales script for everyone to use.

3. Don't waste the call. Offer some great deal that's only available if they buy *now*!

Rating: 3/5

Keep Good Data on Clients

Why stop at their name, address, and phone number? If you ask, you're likely to get their birthdays, spouse's name, mobile number, favorite restaurant, number of children, income, and more. You can use this information to better target your special offers. A good way to get this information is to ask your customers to complete a survey, and offer them a gift voucher as a token of appreciation.

Hints and Tips:

1. The only way to get really valuable information is to *ask*!

2. Offer a gift as an inducement to tell you more about themselves.

3. Make them feel that you are doing this as a favor to them.

Rating: 4/5

Offer Free Trials

When you have a new product *(or even an old one)*, why not let your customers take it home and try it for free? Not only will you get plenty of feedback on it *(and a handful of testimonials)*, you're likely to sell tons. Your customers are naturally predisposed to buying from you, and letting them try something free is usually all the bait they need.

Hints and Tips:

1. Make sure they know how to get the best out of the product.

2. The day before it's due back, tell them they can keep it, 20 percent cheaper than retail! You might build this margin into the original price.

3. Keep in contact during the trial period to ensure that the product hasn't just been put under the bed.

Rating: 4/5

Train Your Team

Run regular training sessions, and let your team members share different ways they've discovered that make clients happy. If they're "not the sort of people to do that kind of thing," give them a pink slip and get some new team members!

Hints and Tips:

1. Encourage feedback from your team members.

2. Get everyone to share what worked, and what didn't.

3. Encourage the sales team members to further their knowledge with courses and seminars, and don't be afraid to pay for it.

4. Encourage a climate where it's OK to criticize constructively.

Rating: 5/5

Offer Big Customers a Shareholding in Your Company

This isn't as complex as it sounds. Ask your accountant how it's done. If a customer gives you the majority of your business, it makes perfect sense to make sure you never lose her business. Once you have your customers as shareholders, they will always buy from you, and they'll probably insist that their friends do as well.

Hints and Tips:

1. Make sure the customer has the potential to make it viable.

2. Ensure that your goals and personalities match.

3. Get professional advice up front to avoid any nasty disputes.

Rating: 3/5

Sell More Consumables

If you just sell the main product, and let someone else sell the consumables, you're missing out. Of course, consumables are often discounted significantly, so you'll need to give people other reasons to buy from you: convenience, expertise, and deals (not discounts).

Hints and Tips:

1. Advertise yourself as the *complete service*.

2. Sell customers on the fact that your consumables are guaranteed to work with the product—others may actually damage it.

3. Offer a package deal on consumables when people buy the original product.

Rating: 3/5

Timetable of Communication

Either rolling or calendar. Rolling is where people are communicated with sequentially. The sequence starts from the moment they buy from you. Calendar is where everyone gets the same thing depending on the time of year. Rolling can work better, as it's more personalized, although calendar is far easier to administer.

Hints and Tips:

1. Make sure your communication with customers is systematized—don't leave it to chance.

2. Rolling communication suits big-ticket items that require personalized correspondence.

3. Calendar communication is more for lower-priced commodity items that are driven by the seasons.

Rating: 5/5

Your Five Killer Number of Transactions Strategies

It's now time to consider the proven ideas of increasing the number of transactions your customers do with you and evaluating them in relation to your own particular situation. As with the other strategies, all may work for you, but which will you try first?

Some of them will be new to you, others not. But which are you making use of regularly already? I don't mean which do you use now and then, or which do you use when you remember. What I mean is which are you using in a systematized way? Which form part of your business routine? You see, it's of no use to you if you're using some of these strategies on a hit-and-miss basis. You

---

NUMBER OF TRANSACTIONS

Strategy 1: _____ Date: _____
Notes: _____
_____
_____
_____

Strategy 2: _____ Date: _____
Notes: _____
_____
_____
_____

Strategy 3: _____ Date: _____
Notes: _____
_____
_____
_____

Strategy 4: _____ Date: _____
Notes: _____
_____
_____
_____

Strategy 5: _____ Date: _____
Notes: _____
_____
_____
_____

---

won't be able to test and measure them in that case, and you won't be able to come to any definitive conclusions as to their effectiveness.

So, right now it's time to put strategies in place that will increase the average number of transactions you currently enjoy.

Identify the five killer number of transaction strategies you think most appropriate to your business right now.

Select the five you'd like to run with first, and write the names of the strategies down on the transactions form on the previous page. Next to each strategy fill in the date by which each is to be implemented.

This page, together with those for the previous parts of the Business Chassis, is adding to the development of your complete and comprehensive *25 killer marketing strategies* and to your *instant marketing plan.*

Average Dollar Sale

This is less of a mystery to most business owners, but precious little is usually done to increase it.

Some customers might spend $500 while others $23.50. The average dollar sale is just that: the *average* dollar spent from everyone who does business with you. All you need to do is divide what's in the till with the number of transactions you've made. I'll show you how to work this out shortly.

Just like McDonald's employees always ask, "Would you like fries with that?" you need to look for ways of increasing your average dollar sale. Even though most people say *no* to the fries, think of the millions of extra dollars they make a day from those that say *yes*. Now think of how a similar strategy could unlock another gold mine for you.

The key is remembering that it only takes slight improvements to make a drastic difference in your profitability. These customers are already doing business with you, and any little extra you can add on is all icing on the cake.

Getting a handle on your average dollar sale is not that difficult to do. In fact, it's very simple. Here's how:

1. Design a simple survey form.

2. Give it to all your salespeople or checkout people and get them to fill it in each day for a limited period—let's say a week.

3. Collate the forms and do the calculation.

This is what your survey form could look like:

AVERAGE DOLLAR SALE SURVEY

Date: _____ Salesperson: _____

CUSTOMER #   **DOLLARS SPENT**

_____   _____

_____   _____

_____   _____

_____   _____

_____   _____

_____   _____

_____   _____

_____   _____

_____   _____

_____   _____

_____   _____

DAILY SUMMARY

No. of Customers: _____

Total Dollars Spent: _____

Average Dollar Sale for the Day: _____
(Total Dollars ˜ No. of Customers)

Once you've completed this simple survey, you'll have an idea of the average dollar sale you're achieving at present. Now you'll know what you have to improve. And you'll know when you've reached your objective. All you have to do now is decide what you've got to do to get there.

There are subtle and not so subtle ways of doing it. Here's the complete repertoire for you to choose from:

49 Tips for Boosting Your Average Dollar Sale
Increase Your Prices

The most obvious way to increase your average dollar sale is to raise your prices. This method should be approached with some caution, although most often you will have more fears about a price rise than any of your customers. If you intend to increase your prices substantially, it's best to gradually phase the new prices in over a period of time.

Hints and Tips:

1. Add 10 percent across the board today.

2. For big rises, phase them in slowly.

3. When you get the 5 to 10 percent of people who object, shift their focus to the quality of your product and the benefits it offers.

4. Check what the competition is charging.

5. Be prepared to offer a little extra service and follow-up.

Rating: 5/5 +++

Up-Sell

This can be done when you have a basic and a deluxe version of a particular product. It works by selling your customers a more expensive version of the product they're looking at, based on its benefits. When upselling it's important to explain how the more expensive model will better suit their long-term needs.

Hints and Tips:

1. Clearly spell out the *benefits* of the more expensive option.

2. Put the price into perspective: "Sure it might be a little more now, but in the long run."

3. Keep your options open. Don't oversell the more expensive product, as someone may be on a very tight budget.

Rating: 5/5

Cross or Add-on Sell

This is a technique that is successfully used by many large companies (see the previous discussion of McDonald's). It can be very effective when selling products or services that are used in conjunction with others. A good example of this would be selling your customers a watering system when they buy a quantity of lawn seed. Or try buying a suit without the sales assistant asking you to try a vast array of ties. You can also cross sell associated products or services on a commission basis with another company.

Hints and Tips:

1. Always offer more than your customers are initially looking for.

2. Offer a package deal if they buy something else as well.

3. Don't overpressure people; after all, you want them to come back.

Rating: 5/5

Down-Sell

Show them the highest-priced item first, and then the one just a little more expensive than they'd originally had in mind will seem extremely cheap. This can be really effective when customers can't afford more expensive items. Rather than attempting to sell them only a higher-priced item, and as a result losing the sale altogether, you simply sell them a similar product that fits just above their budget.

Hints and Tips:

1. Wait until you are absolutely sure that they can't afford the premium product; you just might sell the most expensive item each time.

2. Try and make it sound as though there is little difference between the two products anyway.

3. If you haven't got a cheaper version, try and sell them something else.

Rating: 4/5

Use a Checklist

Similar to add-on selling, you simply run through a checklist with your clients whenever they purchase a particular type of product. This list should be prepared in advance and used with as many different products as possible. For example, if customers buy a can of paint, run through the list to see if they need brushes, thinners, drop sheets, stirrers, etc.

Hints and Tips:

1. Make sure every team member has the list.

2. Check to make sure it's being used with every customer.

3. Have a reward system in place that acknowledges team members who make additional sales off the list.

4. Test and measure. If it is not working change the questions.

Rating: 5/5

Use a Questionnaire

Dig as deep as you can. Make sure you ask enough questions to leave no stone unturned. The more questions you ask, the more chance you have of finding another need or want that you can fill.

Also, if you're unsure of any additional products or services that you could sell, a simple questionnaire can be effective. Use it to ask your customers what else they would like you to sell. Don't limit yourself too much. Ask the customers to get a little creative—who knows, there could be a whole new opportunity just waiting to be suggested.

Hints and Tips:

1. Make your questionnaire simple but effective as a sales tool.

2. Offer customers an incentive to participate, or just explain how what you're doing will help them.

3. Fill it out on the spot with your acting as a sounding board; don't be afraid to ask more questions to dig deeper.

4. Ask for their suggestions, and act as quickly as possible.

Rating: 3/5

Allow Payment Terms or Financing

This allows your customers to spend more by giving them the chance to pay it off over a period of time. You'll find this is particularly beneficial if you're upselling them to a product that's beyond their original budget.

Hints and Tips:

1. Ensure that they are creditworthy.

2. Use it as a real selling tool to close the deal.

3. Ask, "How much can you afford a month?" and then work out a payment plan to suit them—this makes it very hard to say *no*.

Rating: 4/5

Carry Exclusive Lines

By stocking items that can't be purchased elsewhere, you can charge higher than normal prices. The advantage is that your customers can't shop around and get cheaper quotes. This is a great way to avoid C- and D-grade customers asking you for a discount.

Hints and Tips:

1. If people won't pay your price, let them go—other customers will.

2. Exclusivity is worth a lot, so don't be afraid to raise your prices.

3. Use the uniqueness of your product as a selling tool—people love to have something others don't.

Rating: 4/5

Rearrange Store Layout and Merchandising

Make sure your products are on shelving that's clearly marked with bin labels. Not only will that assist your customers when purchasing, but it will also help you when reordering stock.

Stock should be presented clearly with no broken packaging. Fast-moving items should be placed on or just above eye level, with slow-moving items placed just below eye level. End-aisle displays should tell a story with add-on sale items clearly visible.

Make sure your most expensive items, or items with the highest margin, are in your highest traffic areas.

Hints and Tips:

1. Top-selling items should be displayed at eye level.

2. Slower-moving items just below eye level.

3. Make sure all products are clearly marked and cleanly displayed.

4. End aisles should be harnessed with *specials* and impulse products.

Rating: 3/5

Point-of-Sale Material

These take the form of shelf talkers and bin labels and are available from your suppliers. If your current supplier isn't providing you with these "silent salespeople," then call and request that they do. If you're making up your own point-of-sale signs, remember to focus on the benefits of the product. Including a list of accessories that are commonly purchased with that item can help boost sales. For example, if you've got a special on ravioli, it's vital you mention what sauces are available.

Hints and Tips:

1. Sell the benefits, not just the features.

2. Make the signs clear and colorful.

3. List other products that could (should!) be bought along with the original purchase.

Rating: 4/5

Impulse Buys

Place impulse items like chocolates or magazines at cash registers to tempt people as they wait. The longer they wait, the greater chance of their weakening. Impulse buys can also be placed throughout the store. For example, flashlights next to batteries, mops with buckets, and paintbrushes with paint.

Hints and Tips:

1. Always have something tantalizing on offer where people have to wait.

2. Make it a special offer so people think, "Why not?"

3. Class the products together so there's a chance of multiple purchases.

Rating: 4/5

Sell with an Either/Or Question

When you're about to finalize the deal, ask your clients if they would like either the red one or the blue one, delivery on Wednesday or Thursday, if they'll pay by check or credit card. Always give people a choice between one way or another. Never ask a question that can be answered by a *yes* or *no*, because chances are they'll say *no*. Assume they're going to buy; just ask a detail-oriented question to confirm their purchase.

Hints and Tips:

1. Give them two, or in some cases even three, options to choose from.

2. Word the question in such a way that *no* isn't an option—it's just a matter of which one.

3. Remember to ask, "Is there anything else you need?"

Rating: 5/5

Create Package Deals

An excellent way to move more items and increase your average dollar sale is to offer them at a group rate to customers who buy them as part of a package deal. Simply package up a number of associated products and sell them at a price that is less than they would cost individually, but higher than your average dollar sale. You can also use this to sell slow-moving items by including them as part of the deal.

Hints and Tips:

1. Look to package products that complement each other.

2. Try to include products that don't move as well on their own.

3. Make it time sensitive: "This deal is only available today."

Rating: 4/5

Create Bulk Buy Deals

This can be an effective way to encourage people to buy more than they really need right now. Offer your customers a reduced price if they buy a minimum quantity of a particular item.

Hints and Tips:

1. Focus on the convenience of having plenty of product on hand.

2. Be careful not to compromise your margins.

Rating: 4/5

Gift with Minimum Purchase

Offer your clients a gift if they exceed a minimum expenditure. For example, get a free lesson when you buy any new set of golf clubs. This gift shouldn't cost you much but should look as if the client is getting a great deal.

Hints and Tips:

1. Look for a low-cost item or service with a high-*perceived* value.

2. Include the fact that you're giving a gift in all your advertising.

3. Make it time sensitive.

Rating: 4/5

Allow Credit Cards, Debit Cards, and Checks

This is one of the most important facilities you can offer. This can increase your average dollar sale by allowing customers to spend more than they have in their wallets. Credit cards in particular are helpful if you're trying to upsell. If they can have the better model and not have to pay for it right away, they'll take it more often than not.

Hints and Tips:

1. Make it as easy as possible for people to buy.

2. If you're using an electronic payment system, make sure you have the old manual credit card unit available in case of a communication or power failure.

Rating: 5/5

Make Sure Clients Know Your Full Product and Service List

The more they know about, the more they can buy. Place signs around your business to inform your customers of the things you do. Include it in your mailouts, newsletters, and telephone-on-hold messages. It is also important that your sales team members educate the customers on these products/services as they serve them. Most business owners mistakenly assume that their customers know about everything they sell. The fact is they're usually aware of less than one quarter of everything you sell.

Hints and Tips:

1. Tell people what you do and sell, and then tell them again and again.

2. Ensure that all sales team members know as much as you do about the products and services you offer.

3. Have a system in place so sales team members are required to tell customers everything you do, every time.

Rating: 4/5

Charge Consulting Fees

This is a great way to increase your average dollar sale. This works particularly well in the DIY business where many of your customers may not know how to do particular projects. Once you've sold them the products they require, explain to them that you also offer consultations at a minimal cost. And when you're doing your consultation with them, you'll have the chance to sell them extra products.

Hints and Tips:

1. Sell yourself as the expert: "If you want to get the absolute best out of this product, I can show you how."

2. Be careful—with expensive items customers will expect this information free of charge.

3. Use the time together to sell other products. After all, you're the expert.

Rating: 3/5

Sell Service Contracts

When selling a product that needs regular maintenance, you should make use of service contracts. This means that your customers will have all the servicing of their products done by you. Arrange this at the time of purchase for best results. Remember to offer one-, two-, and five-year contracts so that they at least take the one-year contract.

Hints and Tips:

1. Try and make the follow-up appointments at the time of purchase.

2. Take the initiative—if you don't hear from them, call them.

3. Make it part of a special deal and use it to help close the sale.

4. Explain to your customers that the warranty will be void if they don't come back to you for repairs and service.

Rating: 4/5

Sell Extra Warranty or Insurance

An easy way to gain more wallet share. When your customers make a purchase, ask them if they would like to get an extended warranty. Your customers may well jump at the chance to buy that extra peace of mind, particularly on major purchases. This must be done at the time of sale.

Hints and Tips:

1. Do the numbers and make sure it's profitable—it almost always is.

2. Make it sound like a special offer.

3. Do it at the point of sale.

Rating: 3/5

Train Your Team

This is possibly the least utilized marketing tool in business. By training your team on how to up-sell and on-sell products, you can dramatically increase your average dollar sale. Your sales team needs to know your products inside and out. This will make customers feel more comfortable when making a major purchase, knowing that they're dealing with professionals.

Hints and Tips:

1. Constantly educate sales team members about what you offer and how it works.

2. On the technical front, sales team members should know as much as you.

3. Have a reward system in place that encourages sales team members to upsell. Remember, these sales are like the icing on the cake.

4. Think of the time you spend training your sales team as one of the best investments you can make.

Rating: 5/5

Use Sales Scripts

Sales scripts work extremely well when used correctly. They must be used by every salesperson, every time. An example would be to say, "Hi. Have you been in here before?" instead of "Hi. Can I help you?" The first question starts a conversation whereas the second prompts a "No, I'm just looking" answer 90 percent of the time. Scripts should include add-on products that your customers may need to go with their original purchase.

Hints and Tips:

1. Train everyone to use scripts every time.

2. Spend time analyzing what scripts work best, then be prepared to change them.

3. Remember that scripts aren't just for telemarketing. There should be a standard form of interaction every time a customer calls or comes into contact with your business.

Rating: 5/5

Train Your Customers

You need to educate your customers about any additional products and services that you offer. You also need to train them to keep coming back to your store. This can be done by keeping in touch with them and providing a level of service that no one else can offer.

Hints and Tips:

1. Make sure customers are constantly informed about what you do and what you offer.

2. If you start doing anything differently, tell them immediately.

3. Consistent contact is a must.

4. Customers should know that regular patronage will be rewarded.

5. Offer a gift or special discount if they refer a friend to you.

Rating: 4/5

Stock More High-Priced Ranges

This gives you the chance to upsell from your existing budget range. You may decide to drop the cheaper range altogether some time in the future. Care should be taken, as changing your target market can sometimes backfire.

Hints and Tips:

1. Always have extra high-margin products available for those with money to spend.

2. Analyze the profitability of both high- and lower-priced products. It may be prudent to just focus on the premium product.

Rating: 4/5

Create a Quality Image

Present your store and your team members as being professional and upscale. This will eliminate the bargain hunters to a large extent and will allow you to stock more expensive and profitable goods. Both your store and your team need to look immaculate at all times.

Hints and Tips:

1. Make sure your team members dress well—a smart uniform may be needed.

2. Reward team members who constantly present themselves impeccably.

3. Have someone in charge of keeping your premises perfectly clean at all times. This shouldn't be left to chance.

Rating: 3/5

Service Only A-Grade Customers

It has often been said that 80 percent of a company's sales come from 20 percent of the company's customers. An A-grade customer will usually spend more money and be less hassle than other grades of customers. By providing exceptional service for those people you want to do business with, you will encourage them to keep coming back.

Hints and Tips:

1. Know who your best customers are.

2. Treat them like royalty every time.

3. Think of them in terms of lifetime value.

4. Offer gifts and rewards for continued patronage, and encourage them to bring their friends.

Rating: 5/5

Sack C- and D-Grade Customers

Send a letter to any customers that you don't want to do business with. These customers are normally the most demanding of your time, hassle you on price, and then consistently make late payments—and they usually don't need any encouragement to bring their C- and D-grade friends either. In your letter politely and simply outline the minimum standards that you expect from your clients. This way they can either toe the line or go elsewhere.

Hints and Tips:

1. Don't say "go away," but make it clear what you are prepared to accept and what you aren't. They should get the message.

2. Remember that *any* customer isn't necessarily a *good* customer. Some actually cost you money, and worse, take your focus from the A graders.

Rating: 5/5

Allow Trade-ins/Trade-ups

By allowing trade-ins you solve your customers' problem of what to do with the old product. It will also give them the chance to fit that new purchase into their budget. Offering trade-ins means you have the chance to upsell your customers to a better model.

Hints and Tips:

1. Tell the world: Trade-ins get people interested.

2. Make sure you can off-load the trade-ins at a handy profit.

3. Use it as a way of making a more expensive product seem affordable.

Rating: 3/5

Offer Home Delivery

Another way to make it easy for people to deal with you is by offering home delivery. Charging a fee for this service is a great way to increase your average dollar sale. This can prove very popular with larger items such as home furnishings.

Hints and Tips:

1. Cover your cost with a small fee—people will pay for the convenience.

2. For big-ticket items try and include *free delivery* in your advertising.

3. Only deal with a reputable deliverer—damaged products are a nightmare.

Rating: 3/5

Charge for Delivery, Postage, and Packaging

As with home delivery, you simply offer to package and mail items to the customer for a fee. Most people couldn't be bothered doing it themselves and will be happy to pay you to do it. This works best with gift items or products that are difficult to transport.

Hints and Tips:

1. Get a great deal from a delivery company by buying their services in bulk.

2. Don't be afraid to charge extra—people put a high price on convenience these days.

3. Package the product with care. Damaged products leave a sour taste in the customer's mouth, and the extra cost of replacing/fixing comes straight from your pocket (unless you are insured, but then there's the excess).

Rating: 4/5

Build Rapport and Treat as Special

By using simple techniques like always calling your clients by their first names, you will build rapport and trust. Of course the more they trust you, the more you can convince them to buy.

Hints and Tips:

1. Get to know your customers—this starts by listening.

2. Always refer to them by name. If you have a bad memory, organize a card system.

3. Don't always talk business. By getting personal with a customer, you start building trust.

Rating: 4/5

Set and Measure an Average-Dollar-Sale Goal

Set average-dollar-sale goals for all members of your team. This helps them focus and gives them incentive to upsell. A great way to add further incentive is to keep a running scoreboard of sales. The team member with the highest average dollar sale could be rewarded with two free movie passes or half a day off. Putting goals in place is a surefire way to increase sales.

Hints and Tips:

1. Make your goals and targets clear for everyone to see.

2. Openly display your progress and how each individual is doing.

3. Offer generous rewards to those who meet targets.

Rating: 5/5

Customer Incentives for Bigger Purchases

Offer points or funny money that are given out for each dollar spent. When your clients reach a certain number of points, they can receive a discount off their next purchase. Funny money can be honored as real money that is then used for future purchases, or as mentioned before, you can give a gift with a minimum purchase. The idea is to get your customers to spend more than they normally would just to earn extra points.

Hints and Tips:

1. Always have incentives for people to spend more—it's much cheaper than advertising for new customers.

2. It's best to offer rewards in the form of *funny money*, as it encourages them to come back.

3. Have some fun with it. This way people are more likely to remember it and thus more likely to tell their friends.

Rating: 3/5

Team Incentives for Bigger Sales

Set targets for your team and offer a bonus of some kind for each one achieved. List the different prizes available beside each goal. Running it over the course of a month will keep the enthusiasm high among the team. A free Christmas party or social club function would be great incentives as team goals.

Hints and Tips:

1. Openly communicate your goals with everybody.

2. Make it clear what each individual has to do to make it happen.

3. Monitor the progress in such a way that everyone can keep track.

4. Offer great prizes that fire people up.

5. Make sure the gift doesn't take too much away from your margins.

Rating: 5/5

Stop Discounting

Simply don't discount your prices. This will mean that your sales are returning the highest-possible profit margins. If your customers shop around a lot, you may wish to offer some additional incentives such as free home delivery to assist you in closing the sale. It's important that you educate your customers on the value of doing business with your store.

Hints and Tips:

1. Focus on the benefits and quality of your product, not the price.

2. Offer extra services like home delivery or pay by the month.

3. Don't be afraid to lose the sale—remember the C- and D-grade customer rule.

Rating: 5/5

Add Value

Offer added value services to encourage customers to buy from you. These could be something like a free first service with each used car sold, or half-price Scotch Guarding on lounge chairs. Try offering these only on the deluxe models to entice your customers to spend more.

Hints and Tips:

1. Look for cheap ways you can add value—it's all about *perceived* value.

2. These *extras* should be part of the sales script.

3. The more expensive the product, the more you offer.

Rating: 4/5

Give Away Perceived Value

Give away products or services to make it look like your customers are getting excellent value for money. While these things appear great to your customers, the extra you are offering should have cost you little if anything to provide. In other words, you give away the value of an item, not it's hard cost to you.

Hints and Tips:

1. It's not what you give away, but how important and valuable people believe it to be.

2. Something as simple as "your choice of color" can do the trick.

Rating: 4/5

In-Store Promotions

Run in-store promotions on a regular basis to create interest in products or services people will buy as an add-on, or on impulse. These could take the form of product demonstrations, competitions, or sports personalities live in-store. Different events such as Easter, Christmas, or your store's birthday can be turned into interesting promotions.

Hints and Tips:

1. Always link an in-store promotion with a special offer.

2. Make it time sensitive: *only available today*.

3. Once they go for the promoted product, get their attention focused on everything else you offer.

4. Be different. Check out other people's promotions and then better them. This will make you a real talking point.

Rating: 3/5

Flashing-Light Specials

To run flashing-light specials you need a flashing light or siren. This is then set off to direct people to products that are on sale. The sale should only last for 10–30 minutes. It's best to use flashing-light specials when you have stock you wish to clear, damaged goods, or a new product.

Hints and Tips:

1. The discount must be really impressive.

2. Encourage people to buy the product in bulk.

3. Always introduce them to your other products while they are there.

4. Be careful with the flashing lights and sirens—if you run a really upscale business this might not be for you.

Rating: 4/5

Educate on Value, Not Price

You need to get your client focused on the benefits of the product and not the price. This is very important when dealing with bargain hunters or when selling higher-priced or luxury items. To use it effectively, skip over your customers' price queries by immediately coming back at them with a benefit.

Hints and Tips:

1. Focus on *benefits*, not the price.

2. Turn it around with lines like, "Wouldn't you pay a little extra for the added security?"

Rating: 4/5

Ask People to Buy Some More

This technique is probably the most simple to use. When your customers make a purchase, ask them if they would like to buy a couple of spares to have on hand. This works well with disposable items like shoelaces or lightbulbs. You'll get the best results with this technique if the items you're selling are about to increase in price.

Hints and Tips:

1. Spell out the convenience of having a "few extra on hand."

2. Make it sound as though the product could run out of stock at any time.

3. "It's only available at this price for the rest of the week" is also going to get the customer thinking.

Rating: 4/5

Four-for-the-Price-of-Three Offers

This is a great way to encourage people to buy more than they really need. Once again the best results come from semidisposable items. Almost any business can use this type of promotion. Try getting your suppliers to assist with the cost of the promotion by giving you some free stock.

Hints and Tips:

1. Make sure the margins are there to make it profitable.

2. If possible, pass the cost on to your suppliers.

3. The more disposable the product, the better it usually works.

4. Make it time sensitive.

Rating: 3/5

Buy-One-Get-One-Free Offers

Basically the same as four for the price of three. These promotions can be used to great effect where there's a reasonable markup on most goods, or when you want to clear old stock. It outsells two for the price of one, or half price and 50 percent off, by more than double.

Hints and Tips:

1. Make sure there's plenty of margin.

2. Use it as a puller—once people are interested in this great special, show them what else you've got.

3. Make it time sensitive.

4. Use mostly for clearance items to get the money back from your stock.

Rating: 4/5

In-Store Video Promotions

Play videos to demonstrate the features and benefits of a product that you have on sale. In no time you'll have a group of potential prospects milling around your TV set. Once the group is assembled, your sales team can then move in. This is most effective with power tools and electrical equipment, but can be used to promote any product or service that needs a visual demonstration.

Hints and Tips:

1. Use professional production facilities—a shoddy video reflects badly on your business.

2. Use simple language and let the pictures tell the story.

3. Don't make it too long, as many people will come in halfway through.

4. Even though it can be very educational, keep selling the *benefits*.

Rating: 4/5

Store, Team, and Vehicle Appearance

A professional appearance is one of the most important considerations in marketing your business. This gives your customers the impression that you're a quality organization that takes pride in its service. All team members should be dressed in the same clothes featuring your corporate identity. Your store and company vehicles need to be immaculately presented at all times.

Hints and Tips:

1. Coordinate colors and logos throughout your enterprise so you send out the same message all the time.

2. Choose the color(s) carefully. Different colors have different meanings and effects on people.

3. Continually impress on team members the importance of appearance.

4. Lead from the front. If *your* car and clothes are immaculate, it's easier to tell others to do the same.

Rating: 3/5

Suggest the Most Expensive Item First

Customers may be convinced to buy the more expensive item if you immediately communicate its benefits. You should never assume that your customers want the cheaper product. If they can't afford the more expensive product, you then have the option to sell the lower-priced item.

Hints and Tips:

1. Never leave it to chance. Tell every customer about the best and most expensive product.

2. Don't focus on the price. Instead, relentlessly sell the *benefits*.

3. Don't get too pushy, though. Some people might be on a very tight budget, and you don't want to lose the sale completely.

Rating: 5/5

Provide a Shopping List

This is an extension of the checklist strategy where you actually provide your customers with a list of items they may need to complete a particular project.

You'll find this strategy most effective with hardware stores, photography stores, golf stores, and the like.

Hints and Tips:

1. Keep the checklist brief—only include items with mass appeal.

2. Offer a package deal if they buy more than, say, three things from the shopping list.

3. Get customers to at least peruse the checklist on the spot. It's better still if they can use it to buy more stuff immediately.

4. Don't simply list what you've got on sale—use a line or two to explain the benefits.

5. Include your contact details and some kind of call to action in case they take the shopping list home.

Rating: 4/5

Have a Minimum-Dollar-Order Amount

If you're in a service or trade business where you need to travel to your clients, you should consider a minimum dollar order. Many pizza and fast food stores will not deliver to your home unless you spend a minimum amount of money. This strategy is also a good idea for plumbers or mechanics with a 24-hour service. Some companies also charge a minimum purchase price for people wishing to withdraw money using an electronic payment system. It will turn some people away, but it'll allow you to keep your A-grade clients.

Hints and Tips:

1. Clearly explain why you need to enforce a minimum-dollar-sale amount. When people understand, they won't resent it.

2. Do the numbers and make it as low as possible—remember, you want to make it as easy to buy from you as possible.

3. Be careful with credit/debit. There are very few businesses that have a minimum purchase required these days, and you may look greedy and old fashioned if you have such a policy.

Rating: 3/5

Allow Layaway

This is a great way to get people to buy products that they can't really afford right now and increase your average dollar sale. It has the added advantage of bringing them into your store on a regular basis to make payments. Obviously this gives you the chance to show them any new products that you can attempt to sell them.

Hints and Tips:

1. Make sure you've got the margins to pay for the extra administration.

2. Use it as a selling point in your marketing and promotion—many of your competitors may not be offering it.

3. Look for seasonal surges like Christmas, so you can target people six months from these dates when they are going to want to take delivery of the product.

4. Never miss an opportunity to on-sell when they come in to make payments.

Rating: 3/5

Your Five Killer Average-Dollar-Sale Strategies

Once again, I'm going to get you to consider the proven ideas for increasing your average dollar sale and evaluating them in relation to your own particular situation. As with the other strategies, all may work well for you, but which will you try first?

Some will be more applicable to your business than others. For instance, if you run a PR consultancy, you'd hardly try a red flashing-light sale, would you? Start off by eliminating those that definitely won't suit your business. But before you do, try some lateral thinking first. Can you adapt the idea to suit your situation? If you can, you're almost certain to come up with a unique point of difference. And this will make you stick out from the crowd and attract the attention of your target market. You'll have just set in motion a strategy that has every chance of increasing your average dollar sale.

So, right now it's time to put strategies in place that will do just that.

Identify the five killer average-dollar-sale strategies you think most appropriate for your business right now.

Select the five you'd like to run with first and write the names of the strategies down on the form below. Next to each strategy fill in the date by which each is to be implemented.

This page, together with those for the previous parts of the Business Chassis, is adding to the development of your complete and comprehensive *25 killer marketing strategies*, and your *instant marketing plan*.

AVERAGE DOLLAR SALE

Strategy 1: _____ Date: _____
Notes: _____
_____
_____
_____

Strategy 2: _____ Date: _____
Notes: _____
_____
_____
_____

Strategy 3: _____ Date: _____
Notes: _____
_____
_____
_____

Strategy 4: _____ Date: _____
Notes: _____
_____
_____
_____

Strategy 5: _____ Date: _____
Notes: _____
_____
_____
_____

Profit Margins

Margins are what you make after *all* costs have been deducted.

Therefore, any increase you make to margins is clean profit, and that's got to be a good thing. In fact, profit is my favorite six-letter word.

Yet despite the black-and-white advantages of increased margins, far too little time is spent analyzing ways of improving them.

The really exciting part is that the tiniest of improvements can equate to huge differences in your bank balance. By increasing margins by just 5 percent, some businesses will experience profit increases equivalent to a 50 percent rise in sales—sometimes even more.

Give me a P, give me an R, give me an O, give me an F, give me an I, give me a T: What does it spell? Margins! One last thing: This isn't just about cost cutting; it's far more exciting.

Once again, it will help if you have a fair idea of what your average margin is before you put in place strategies aimed at improving them. Some businesses will have different margins for different products, while others may work on a standard margin across the board. Make a list of yours and include it in this marketing plan. If you have difficulty doing this, ask your accountant or financial controller. You could use a form similar to this:

MARGIN SURVEY

Date: _____

Department or Product Range:	Item:	Margin:
_____	_____	_____
	_____	_____
	_____	_____
_____	_____	_____
	_____	_____
	_____	_____

Obviously the survey form you use should be designed to reflect the type of business you're in. If you run a supermarket, you'd probably want to group all products in a specific category. Dairy products might form one category, while sugar and spices, meat, cleaning products, personal hygiene, and magazines might form others. If you're in the service industry, you might work on a standard across-the-board margin, in which case things become simpler. For instance, a PR agency might have a survey form that reflects different departments such as graphic design, PR, photography, and events management.

It might be more convenient making use of, or adapting, your inventory sheets. You might already have something suitable to use that might well fit in with your current systems or procedures. If this is the case, that's great. If not, now's the time to design something that suits your style of operation. You see, just by going through an exercise like this you will start focusing attention on your margins. By doing nothing more, you could uncover something that looks odd, too low, or not in keeping with what you'd expect.

So, having done that, here's how to rev up the last part of the Business Chassis.

65 Ways to Boost Your Margins
Increase Your Margins/Prices

Most business owners have more of a problem with a price rise than do their customers. This has to be the fastest and best way to jump your profitability. Ninety-five percent of your customers won't even notice the rise, and the 5 percent that do complain are the 5 percent that already complain. Remember, if you're still too scared to increase your prices across the board, just increase the prices on the 80 percent of your products or services that are the slow sellers and leave the 20 percent of your fastest sellers until last.

Hints and Tips:

1. Introduce increases right now.

2. Don't draw attention to the rises, but if people inquire, explain the reason and then focus on the extra benefits.

3. Make it at least a 10 percent price rise.

Rating: 5/5

Sell More Big-Margin Goods/Services

Quite often a lower-priced item will offer a greater margin. You should consider exactly how much each item makes you, and then continue to stock only those that make you the most money. If you work in the service industry, you should consider which services offer the most money for the least amount of effort.

Hints and Tips:

1. Know the exact margins on everything you sell and do.

2. Always shift the customer's focus to high-margin products and services.

3. Only offer services that have high margins—after all, time is money!

Rating: 5/5

No Discounting

If you constantly discount, why have a regular retail price? Discounting not only costs you money, but it gives the impression that your normal prices are a rip-off. Customers may also hold off buying, thinking an item that's $100 today may only be $80 tomorrow. It's better to not discount but instead simply offer more add-on value.

Hints and Tips:

1. Focus on value and benefits instead of haggling over price.

2. Don't set a precedent by discounting—if you do it for one person, others start expecting it.

3. If you do have to discount, make the discounted offer first to your past customers only.

Rating: 5/5

Sell Only Quality

By selling only quality goods and services, you can afford to increase your margins. Best of all you won't need to worry about customers bringing them back to be repaired. When considering the move to higher-quality stock, you need to keep two points in mind. First, the goods still have to be affordable for your existing clients. And second, you must be making more money out of them per sale.

Hints and Tips:

1. Make sure that the higher the price, the higher the margin.

2. Constantly emphasize the quality of the product when dealing with clients.

3. Ensure that your customer base will be able to afford any new offerings.

4. Remember: A quality product must also mean quality service.

Rating: 4/5

Sell Your Own Label

This is guaranteed to increase your slice of the profits. Selling your own label also gives you the chance to discount on certain lines to undercut your opposition. The beauty of this is that because there's no middleman, you're probably still making more profit than your opposition would be at full price.

Hints and Tips:

1. Manufacture only simple products that aren't constantly afflicted with delivery problems and budget overruns.

2. Only discount your brand periodically—you need to build it as a quality brand.

3. Do the figures and weigh it up carefully before commissioning anything.

Rating: 3/5

Sell an Exclusive Label

This gives you the opportunity to increase your margin because your clients simply can't go anywhere else to buy your product. But don't be too greedy. Increase your margin only as much as the market will bear.

Hints and Tips:

1. Look for something special no one else offers.

2. Make the exclusivity factor a feature in your marketing.

3. People will pay extra for something exclusive, so don't be afraid to charge a premium.

Rating: 3/5

Sack C's and D's

These clients tend to take up a lot of time and are slow in paying their accounts. You'll find that these clients will normally want a discounted rate that ultimately affects your profit margins. Simply send them a letter explaining the way you're now doing business and that they have to pay full price, on time, every time, so you can continue to deliver the level of service you do.

Hints and Tips:

1. Evaluate every client—some aren't worth keeping.

2. C's and D's take far too much of your time away from the real gold mine; your A's, and to a lesser extent, your B's.

3. When sending the letter, leave the door open for them to come back, but only if they follow the rules.

Rating: 4/5

Keep an Accurate Database

If your database is out-of-date you can waste a lot of time and money contacting inactive customers, or sending mail to an old address after your clients have moved. By regularly updating your database you can be sure that your time and money is being well spent.

Hints and Tips:

1. Constantly monitor and update all your contacts.

2. Not only could you be sending material to the wrong person, but the intended recipient *(who's a great prospect)* receives nothing.

3. Assign someone to carry out this job—don't leave it to chance.

Rating: 3/5

Sell via Direct Mail and the Internet

This is a great way to lower overheads and other expenses such as wages and advertising costs. By using these mediums you're able to operate from home, simply taking orders and mailing out the goods. Selling by mail order reduces your overheads and thus gives you a much higher slice of the profits.

Hints and Tips:

1. Get great lists or e-mail addresses—it's worth the initial investment.

2. You must have a fantastic offer.

3. Test and measure so you come up with a great headline.

4. The letter or e-mail should be short, concise, and full of *selling* words describing the benefits.

Rating: 3/5

Sell via Party Plan or MultiLevel

Another way to lower overheads is to sell party plans or via multilevel marketing. This also allows you to operate from home with minimal overheads. You're effectively recruiting people to sell your product for you, without paying them a wage. You also travel to their homes so you don't need to spend money turning your home into an office.

Hints and Tips:

1. Study how other systems work and ask, "Could this work with my business?"

2. The product should preferably be unique and always of top quality.

3. There needs to be plenty of margin.

4. The commission structure must be very generous so people are motivated to sell.

Rating: 3/5

Commission-Only Sales Team

One of the greatest burdens on any business is that of team costs. Vacation pay, insurance, and sick days are all examples of wasted money that comes with paying wages. By employing salespeople on commission only, you can avoid many of these unnecessary costs. You have the added benefit of knowing that your team members have to perform to survive. If they don't make sales, you don't pay them. This way you can be sure your company is not carrying any unwanted passengers.

Hints and Tips:

1. This is the safest way to run a business: pay on performance.

2. The commissions need to be terrific.

3. It's a great way of testing people, as they usually leave voluntarily if they don't perform.

Rating: 5/5

Provide Team Training

By ensuring that your team is multiskilled you can cut down on costs. Holidays become less of a concern, as other team members are then able to cover. You may also find that you need to outsource less of your work and can better utilize the time of your existing team.

Hints and Tips:

1. Training team members is one of the best investments you can make.

2. By multiskilling your team, you become far less reliant on individuals who may get sick or leave.

3. Constantly encourage team members to broaden their skills base.

4. Make sure at least two people within your organization know how to do any given task.

Rating: 4/5

Pay *No* Overtime

This should be negotiated with your team members when you discuss their employment agreements. Rather than pay them overtime, you can perhaps negotiate flextime or some other suitable system. Many employees may actually prefer this system because overtime puts them into a higher tax bracket. It's important that you realize that any overtime you're paying is significantly cutting into your profits.

Hints and Tips:

1. Plan well and try to do everything during business hours.

2. Instead of overtime, give team members the time off when business is quieter.

3. Speak to team members and organize a suitable trade-off that doesn't involve exorbitant rates.

Rating: 4/5

Reduce Team Size

With careful evaluation of your systems, you may be able to reduce the size of your team without losing productivity. In many cases you'll find that some of your team members have long periods of inactivity during the day. By eliminating some of your team you can get the most out of those remaining, and cut down on your wages bill.

Hints and Tips:

1. Closely analyze the output of each individual.

2. Simply give team members more work and see if they cope.

3. Embrace any new technology that is making the workplace much more efficient than in the past.

Rating: 4/5

Reduce Unnecessary Management

Improving your team training can assist in this area. Many modern businesses suffer from top-heavy management levels. By putting systems into place and improving the training of your team, it may be possible to make some of the management positions in your company obsolete.

Hints and Tips:

1. Learn to delegate power to those on the front lines.

2. Develop systems that allow employees to work unsupervised.

3. Reward those that work unsupervised for meeting goals—this can be a lot cheaper than paying a manager to drive them.

Rating: 5/5

Reduce Directors' Fees

Simply stop paying yourself so much. Many directors draw excess money out of their companies, and this eventually creates cashflow problems. It is important to have a pool of money so you can pay any unexpected costs that arise, or take advantage of investment opportunities. Change directors' fees and take them as profits at the end of the year when you know you can afford to.

Hints and Tips:

1. Leave as much money in the business as possible.

2. For tax reasons it's often best to reinvest your earnings.

Rating: 3/5

Efficiency, Productivity, and Time Management

These are three areas that can be responsible for large sums of wasted money. If you evaluate each of these areas individually, you can quickly identify which of them is costing you money. Notifying your team members of the minimum performance standards that's expected of them can help to fix any problems.

Hints and Tips:

1. Analyze each area separately.

2. Clearly spell out what's expected of team members in each area.

3. Reward those who meet and exceed goals.

Rating: 4/5

Negotiate Employment Agreements

This is one area where savings can be made quickly. Eliminating overtime and holiday loadings are examples of achievable goals that can be successfully negotiated. But it's important to remember that in order to attract and keep good people, you must offer them something worthwhile.

Hints and Tips:

1. Negotiate every contract as though it were a business deal.

2. Find out what motivates the team—it might not necessarily be money!

3. Try and reduce the base salary as much as possible while increasing the profit performance bonus. This makes it safer for you and it increases motivation.

Rating: 4/5

Team Incentives Based on Margins

Why should you be the only person concerned with margins? Your team members can assist you in boosting your margins, particularly if you make it worth their effort. So, offer them an incentive based on margins. An example of this would be if you had standard and discount prices. Simply pay your sales team members a higher commission on anything they sell at the full price. This will allow you to fix your margins, not just your commission percentages.

Hints and Tips:

1. All team members need a clear understanding of what the margins are.

2. Offer a larger percentage reward for sales made at full margin.

3. Spell out the numbers—your sales team members need to know at what level their commission stops.

Rating: 5/5

Reduce Duplication

By cutting down on double handling and unnecessary paperwork, you can save your company thousands of dollars. Take the time to look at your existing systems to see if there's any area that is guilty of duplication. This can easily eliminate wasted time and expense.

Hints and Tips:

1. Constantly audit your systems.

2. Encourage team members to complain about duplication or wasted time spent on paperwork.

3. If feasible, get a third party to look after administration so your sales team has only one concern: to sell.

Rating: 4/5

Know Your Actual Costs

Many of your expenses are never evaluated. If you take some time to find out what your actual costs are, you can then look at ways of reducing them. By getting quotes on different services and products you can save substantial amounts of money.

Hints and Tips:

1. Sit down, spend a weekend, and check everything. And if you haven't got the patience, pay someone to do it for you.

2. Always seek numerous quotes when purchasing anything of an ongoing nature.

Rating: 5/5

Work Costs as a Percentage of Sales

All costs that arise in your business need to be calculated as a percentage of sales. This gives you an idea of how many sales you need to make before you start showing a profit. To do this, work out how much it costs you to run your business each week. You need to include all expenses, from wages to stationery, electricity bills to rent—anything that you have to pay to keep your doors open. Then work out how many sales are needed to cover that cost before you start to see a profit. Once you've identified this figure, explain to your team members what is required to keep the business profitable. This will motivate them to increase sales and achieve their goals.

Hints and Tips:

1. Communicate the figure to all team members—they need to know what it takes to stay open.

2. Have a reward system in place that kicks in only after you reach the break-even point.

Rating: 5/5

Set Monthly Expenditure Budgets

This is important if your business is to remain viable. By setting monthly expenditure budgets and then sticking to them, you can make sure that you're never in the situation where your company has more money going out than it has coming in.

Hints and Tips:

1. Set budgets early and then inform everyone what the figures are.

2. The budget should be like the eleventh commandment: not broken under any circumstances.

Rating: 5/5

Allow Your Team to Buy Only with an Authorized Purchase Order

This way you can keep track of any money that's being spent. It isn't necessarily because you don't trust your team, but more to ensure that your money is only being spent on the bare essentials.

Hints and Tips:

1. This is crucial for proper planning and prudent accounting.

2. Tell your team members that it's not about trust, but rather a way of making them ask, "Is this really necessary?"

Rating: 5/5 +++

Better Negotiation Skills

You need to be strong in this area if you want to get the best deals. Everything from employment agreements, to getting the best deals from your suppliers, depends on your skill in this field. Rehearsing in front of a mirror or practicing in the car as you drive can develop these skills. You need to make sure you're getting the best deals from your suppliers so that you're making the maximum profit from selling their products.

Hints and Tips:

1. Be up-front and always ask for discounts.

2. Shop around and use other prices as a negotiation tool.

3. Reverse the whole process. Sell your suppliers on the benefits of doing business with *you*.

4. If suppliers dig their heels in, don't think it's not worth changing. The fact that you are about to leave can be enough to bring them back.

Rating: 5/5

Reduce *All* Costs by 10 Percent

It's not easy but with a bit of effort it is possible to reduce all your costs by at least 10 percent. The first step is to know what they are right now. Some will be easier to reduce than others, but lower overheads mean greater profits, so you need to devote some time to this area. Gaining quotes from a number of suppliers, subcontractors, or freight services are just a few examples of ways to cut costs.

Hints and Tips:

1. Take it one step at a time—just 1 percent a week and within 10 weeks you've made it.

2. Break down each area of your business and attack it individually.

3. Constantly audit all facets of your operation.

4. Consider bringing in an objective outsider for this task.

Rating: 5/5

Do It Right the First Time

You only get paid to do most things once, so if you don't do it right the first time your profits can quickly dwindle. For example, mechanics that make money via an hourly rate will waste much of their profit on a job if they have to redo it. So, taking a bit longer and doing it right once can be well worthwhile.

Hints and Tips:

1. Don't skimp on quality; repairs cost a lot more in the long run.

2. Sure, make mistakes—but only once.

3. Invest in training for yourself and your team members so everyone becomes expert at doing it fast and right the first time.

Rating: 4/5

Recycle

There are many different products you can recycle to help reduce expenses. If you have a photocopier, then use both sides of the paper, or buy refillable ink cartridges for your printer. By taking the time to recycle it's possible to save a considerable amount of money over a period of time.

Hints and Tips:

1. Create a recycling mission statement and hang it proudly.

2. Encourage your team to come up with ideas on recycling—you may even have a "green-thumb" award for standout suggestions.

3. Look around and check what other companies are doing on the recycling front and borrow their ideas.

Rating: 3/5

Decrease Range

The longer an item sits on your shelf, the less profit you will eventually make from it. If you eliminate your slow-moving stock and only carry those lines which sell quickly, you can make more money per item sold. Remember, the greater the range, the more suppliers you have accounts with, the more shelf space you need, the more money you have invested in stocks, the more costs you'll have, and so on.

Hints and Tips:

1. Monitor the movements of every item.

2. Invest more in those items that move quickly.

3. Don't be afraid to sacrifice, at cost, stock that hangs around too long.

4. By buying more fast-moving items you should be able to negotiate bulk deals with your supplier.

5. As a result, you can offer better bulk deals to your customers.

Rating: 5/5

Take Stock on Consignment

This way you don't have to outlay money on stock that could take some time to move. You don't have to pay for it until it sells, which means your money can be working for you elsewhere. This is one of the most effective ways to increase your margins.

Hints and Tips:

1. Make sure there is plenty more stock available if it proves really popular.

Rating: 5/5

Lower Dollars Tied Up in Inventory

You should never have too much stock in inventory. This has an adverse effect on cashflow, and you run the risk of being stuck with it if trends change. Always keep your inventory as low as possible, without running short, and then only order stock as you need it.

Hints and Tips:

1. Have systems in place that alert you the instant stock levels are low.

2. Always carry more stock of the popular items. You only know which ones these are by testing and measuring.

3. Deal only with suppliers who can fulfill your order quickly.

4. If you do run out of stock, offer to give them a temporary *used* or *demo* product until a new one is available.

Rating: 5/5

Sell Only Fast-Moving Stock

Any stock that sits on shelves is wasting money. The longer it sits there, the lower the margin you make on it when it finally goes. If the stock is particularly slow moving it will probably need to be sold at a discounted price. So make sure that you only stock goods that move quickly.

Hints and Tips:

1. Keep tabs on the turnover of each product.

2. If it's a fast mover, promote it even more.

3. If it's a slow mover, dump it.

Rating: 5/5

Buy in Bulk, Pay and Receive over Time

This is a great idea if you've got smaller items that move quickly. Order a bulk quantity from your supplier and then arrange to have X amount delivered each month. You then pay for each shipment as it arrives. This way you don't have to fork out for the whole lot in one hit, allowing you to invest the money elsewhere.

Hints and Tips:

1. Get a commitment from the supplier that the price won't rise.

2. Also establish that if the products don't arrive on time each month, you are entitled to some form of discount.

3. You can also use this technique when selling to your customers, except this time focus on getting a commitment that forces them to pay for what's ordered at the designated times.

Rating: 5/5

Manufacture It Yourself

If you're selling a lot of a particular item, you should look at the possibility of manufacturing it yourself. Obviously the benefit of making it yourself is that you make the maximum profit out of each sale. Instead of your manufacturer's making a lot and your making a bit, you get both slices. This strategy is one well worth looking into.

Hints and Tips:

1. Make sure you know everything about the manufacturing process.

2. Budget very carefully and do the numbers.

3. Works best with high-volume products.

4. Make sure there's enough demand in the marketplace.

5. Sell your product wholesale to your competitors. In the long run this may even be the bulk of your business.

Rating: 3/5

Repackage Smaller with Your Own Label

A lot of your profit can go into the packaging of your product. By buying in bulk and then repackaging into your own label you can significantly increase the margins on each product you sell. To further increase the amount you make on each sale, shop around to get quotes from different packaging companies.

Hints and Tips:

1. Never be satisfied—continually shop around.

2. Ask customers what type and size of packaging they like. Their answers, often suggesting higher-margin alternatives, may surprise you.

Rating: 4/5

Promote Idle Time

If your business is service-based, then this is an area you may need to look at. For companies such as plumbers, mechanics, or accountants, who make their money from charging an hourly rate, promoting idle time is critical. To get clients coming in during quiet periods you should look at offering a reduced rate or additional free service. To operate during these times at a slightly reduced fee is better than not operating at all. Restaurants can even get their past customers back on slower nights with a "Tuesday Night Club."

Hints and Tips:

1. Offer your services at lower rates during lull periods.

2. While doing this work, sell your benefits, and try to secure fully paid work during peak times—you start this by doing a great job.

3. Get creative. Is there an extra service you could be adding to your current repertoire that will get you more attention?

Rating: 3/5

Rent Idle Space

If you've got office, warehouse, or workshop space that's not being used, you should be trying to rent it out. In many cases it's worth the time and expense of renovating the area to make it more attractive. This gives you extra revenue and can be great for business if you get a company in that provides a service that complements yours. An excellent example of this would be for a mechanic to lease an unused section of the workshop to a car detailer.

Hints and Tips:

1. Look for a business that complements yours.

2. You may even be able to entice a strategic alliance partner that will help bring you more business.

3. Keep the lease as flexible as possible—you may need the space back.

Rating: 3/5

Work Two or Even Three Shifts

This is a great idea for any business looking to cut down on the amount of equipment it needs to purchase. For example, a data entry company could run two shifts rather than buying two sets of computers. This eliminates the need to pay overtime as well as saves money on equipment.

Hints and Tips:

1. Look for team members who are willing to work shift hours.

2. Make sure your building has 24-hour access.

Rating: 3/5

Have Smaller Outlets

Redesign your operations so you can run it with much smaller outlets. Or, if you have excess floor space, then you have one of two options. You can either rent the unused space to another business or move to smaller premises. If you're paying for floor space that's not being used (*or not likely to be used any time soon*) move *now*!

Hints and Tips:

1. Constantly monitor the use of floor space.

2. Remember: smaller office doesn't mean smaller business.

3. Look to incorporate open office designs that drastically cut down on floor space.

Rating: 3/5

Work from Home

Many people believe that when they go into business for themselves they must rent an office or storefront. The truth is that many small businesses can be run from home. This cuts down on your overheads and transportation costs, as you don't need to commute to work. You also have the added advantage of paying only one lot of bills and receiving a number of tax benefits. So if working from home is an option, then you should take advantage of it, because lower overheads mean greater profits. Or, go one step further and let your team work from home.

Hints and Tips:

1. If clients visit you, there must be a separate area that looks business-like and professional.

2. Design the office in such a way that you can lock yourself away from the daily distractions of the house.

3. Use of the latest computer and communications technology can make your home office seem very professional to those that don't know where you are located.

4. Make sure you take advantage of all the tax benefits.

Rating: 4/5

Have a Mobile Business

This can be a great one for mechanics and hairdressers in particular. As with working from home, having a mobile business dramatically reduces your overheads. It also offers similar tax benefits and is often more convenient for your customers.

Hints and Tips:

1. Plan your trips so there is minimum travel between each client.

2. Convenience is valuable, so charge extra to go to people's home or places of business.

3. Make convenience central to your advertising and marketing.

4. Be sure to take advantage of all the tax benefits.

Rating: 4/5

Join or Start a Buying Group

If there's one already going, then join it. If not, then start your own. By joining with other companies to form a buying group you can achieve substantial savings in a short period of time. The idea is quite simple. Manufactures offer bulk prices to companies who buy a lot of stock. As individual companies you probably can't buy a large enough volume to get these prices. But if you join together with other companies who also sell these products, your combined purchasing power should enable you to get a better price.

Hints and Tips:

1. Buying in groups gives you immense leverage.

2. Join only with reputable businesses that pay on time.

3. Coordinate your purchases carefully—it's almost always a case of the bigger the order the better the deal.

4. When negotiating with suppliers, constantly remind them that a *no* to you means a *no* to X number of customers.

Rating: 5/5

Refinance

If you have a number of loans, then you need to consolidate them into one. This gives you the advantage of paying only one amount of interest and one repayment. You also need to shop around to find the best interest rate. This doesn't always mean the cheapest, so make sure the one you choose suits your particular needs.

Hints and Tips:

1. Don't just look at the interest rate; the features and benefits are also important considerations.

2. Shop around regularly—there's now fierce competition between the banks, nonbank lenders, and credit unions.

3. Offer the chosen institution all your banking needs—business and personal—in exchange for an even better deal.

4. A solid business plan often makes negotiations easier.

Rating: 5/5

Charge for a Finance Facility

Any business that offers finance to customers should arrange it on a commission basis. Approach a number of loan companies and offer to sell their product for a commission. This is a great way to increase your profits from each sale. You can also charge interest on 30-, 60-, or 90-day accounts. To hide this extra charge you simply offer a discount for accounts paid within seven days. This means that any account that isn't paid in that time is loaded with interest.

Hints and Tips:

1. Look for finance companies that offer you the best margins.

2. This makes it easier for the customer to pay, so tell the world in your advertising and marketing, "Only $75 a month."

3. Include interest charges on accounts that aren't settled by the due date.

4. Clearly inform your customers about the penalties and when they start.

Rating: 4/5

30-Day Terms to 7 Days

Change your accounts from 30 to 7 days. This allows you to earn extra interest on the money to purchase more stock. By doing this you'll improve your cashflow. Remember, the money is always better off in your account.

Hints and Tips:

1. Reward customers who pay early with a gift or small discount.

2. Charge interest on overdue accounts.

3. Have accounting systems that immediately alert you to payments in arrears.

Rating: 5/5

Invest in Technology

This will improve the speed at which your business operates. You need to have the fastest, most reliable machines that you can afford. You should also have all your accounts and files on computer. To manually do any bookkeeping in this day and age is criminal.

Hints and Tips:

1. Set a budget and then buy the best you can afford.

2. Don't worry too much about technology quickly becoming obsolete—eventually you have to dive in.

3. Look for an accounting package that's similar to your accountant's so you can work together electronically.

4. Get on the Internet. You can save a lot of time and money by communicating via e-mail. It also makes you look more professional.

5. Invest in some computer training so you make maximum use of your equipment.

6. Buy from companies that offer solid after-sales support.

Rating: 5/5

Systemize the Routine, Humanize the Exceptions

Basically this means that you should put systems in place to cut down on your team's workload. Effective systems can often make the people who are performing those tasks able to perform them at a higher level and able to perform more tasks in the same amount of time. Make a list of all the routine tasks and write, record on video or audiotape, a system for each and every task. Once again, systemize the routine, humanize the exceptions.

Hints and Tips:

1. Regularly audit all your tasks and ask, "Could this be done better using a different system?"

2. Remember the customer—there are some things that a machine just can't do.

Rating: 5/5 +++

Automate as Much as Possible

Investing in machines to do the work previously done by a team member is a wise choice. By automating, you not only save money on wages, you can also increase your productivity. This means that your goods will cost less to produce and, therefore, give you a greater profit margin. So, always look at putting a system in place rather than employing more people.

Hints and Tips:

1. The initial up-front investment in machines can quickly pay itself off if they are utilized properly.

2. Make sure you get complete training in their use.

3. A strong warranty and after-sales follow-up is a must.

4. Explain to team members why the changes are necessary, and only keep those who are willing to embrace technology.

Rating: 4/5

Sell Obsolete Equipment/Machinery

Printers and dry cleaners are notorious for keeping outdated equipment. Any old piece of machinery that you have should be sold to generate extra revenue. The profit from the sale of old equipment can be used to offset the cost of a new replacement.

Hints and Tips:

1. Never unnecessarily hang onto obsolete equipment.

2. Try and find a supplier who will accept it as trade-in on new equipment.

3. If you can't get a trade-in, sell it complete or as spare parts.

4. Plan old equipment sales and upgrades so you get the best possible tax benefits.

Rating: 3/5

Sell Off Old Stock

It's not making you any money sitting in a storeroom, and if it's on a shelf then it's taking up space that could be occupied by a more profitable item. Selling off your old stock at cost or above creates extra revenue and allows you to display faster-moving goods with greater margins.

Hints and Tips:

1. Do regular inventories and *fire sale* old and slow-moving items.

2. Maybe offer them as a special deal, in bulk, or simply give them away with purchases of your higher-margin products.

3. Don't buy these items again.

Rating: 4/5

Reduce or Eliminate Taxation Expense

For this you need to find an accountant who is financially literate. And no, just because the accountant is qualified doesn't mean that he knows how to reduce your tax expense. There are many ways in which a top accountant can minimize your tax burden, so it's worth taking the time to find one.

Hints and Tips:

1. Don't hire the first accountant you call. Do some serious interviewing and shopping around.

2. Ask business associates, family, and friends what accountant they use and why.

3. Get references from other clients *(if confidentially issues allow it)* and check their track record.

4. Ask a prospective accountant the tough questions—don't be intimidated.

5. If you don't like the service you are getting now, it's worth the hassle to leave. A good accountant can save you a fortune.

Rating: 5/5

Negotiate Fixed Expenses

If you use a particular service on a regular basis, then you should consider arranging a fixed rate. For example, if a business needs to have its computers serviced four times a month, and the fee was $120 per service, it would be worthwhile arranging to pay a retainer of $160 per month and $60 per service. This can be applied to any regular service you use.

Hints and Tips:

1. Lock in suppliers you use on a regular basis. This ensures continuity of service and price predictability.

2. Emphasize your *lifetime value* to them and negotiate from there.

3. Get as many quotes as possible. This gives you a much better bargaining position.

Rating: 4/5

Employ People In-House

This is a great way for you to reduce your expenses and increase your margins. In many cases it's far less expensive to pay somebody a wage than it is to subcontract the work out. A good example would be a business that regularly uses the services of a graphic designer. If the hourly rate for subcontract work was $70, and the designer could be employed to work full-time for $24 per hour, then employing in-house would make more sense.

Hints and Tips:

1. Do some monthly figures and compare those hours at *outsource* and *wage* rates.

2. When analyzing the figures, remember that someone working for you full time will have many extra overheads like workers' compensation, sick leave, holidays, retirement, etc.

3. If you do hire someone, start her on a three-month trial period so you don't get stuck with a bad apple.

Rating: 3/5

Outsource

It is not always less expensive to employ workers in-house. If you don't have enough work to keep them busy full time, or if the cost of the equipment they need is too great, you're better off outsourcing the work.

Hints and Tips:

1. For sporadic work, outsourcing is the way to go.

2. If you use people regularly, try and negotiate down their price.

3. Make sure they have all the equipment necessary to complete the task.

4. Set strict deadlines with penalties of nonpayment so they don't get distracted with other jobs.

Rating: 3/5

Move Premises

This should be considered for a couple of reasons. First, if you need to ship your goods over a long distance, then moving could save you the cost of transportation. Another reason would be to save money on rent. This is a good idea for any business that doesn't rely on passing traffic.

Hints and Tips:

1. You should be located in the area where you do most business.

2. If you don't need to make a great impression with your premises, go for practicality instead of panache.

3. For those not relying on passing traffic, look to set up somewhere like an industrial area where the rent is much cheaper.

4. Calculate carefully how much room you need and then don't commit to any more.

5. Use open office design to cut down on space.

Rating: 4/5

Pay Cash Rather than Loan Interest

Any interest you're currently paying on loans is wasted money. You need to get your loans paid off and then pay cash for future orders. This could take some time but you'll benefit in the long run.

Hints and Tips:

1. If you've got the cash, use it!

2. See if you can make periodic interest-free payments. Push this harder with regular suppliers.

3. Consolidate your loans so you only pay one set of fees and a better, negotiated interest rate.

4. Think of credit cards as a convenience, not a source of long-term capital.

Rating: 5/5

Buy Only What You *Need*

Having an excess of stock reduces your company's cashflow. You should only carry a minimum amount of stock and then order more when you start to run low. You should also keep everyday costs down by buying only things like stationery items if they're absolutely essential.

Hints and Tips:

1. Be ruthless—only stock what you really need.

2. Plan ahead. Things like stationery should be getting home delivered these days.

3. Planning also ensures that you don't make a mad dash to the convenience store and pay three times too much for an item.

Rating: 5/5

Use a Company Credit Card for Bonus Points and up to 55 Days Interest Free

Use a company credit card rather than paying by check. This way you can leave the money in your account for up to 55 days earning interest, or direct it into other investments. Using your credit card can also gain you benefits such as airline bonus points. These points can be accumulated and then used later for business trips.

Hints and Tips:

1. Get a card with long interest-free payback periods.

2. Remember to pay on time, as one day overdue can bring heavy penalties.

3. Check the reward point structure and go with the best.

4. If your supplier won't take credit cards, go somewhere else.

5. Paying by card also helps with your accounting as you get all the expenditures monthly on a single statement.

Rating: 4/5

Rent for Maximum Tax Write-Off

Renting is a great way to gain tax exemptions. If you own the building you work in, it will be classed as an asset and cannot be claimed. However, if you rent the building, it becomes an expense that can then be claimed. Saving money on your tax will help make your business more profitable.

Hints and Tips:

1. Don't think of rent just as "dead money." There can be some significant tax savings involved.

2. If you own commercial property, speak with your accountant and ensure that it wouldn't be more profitable to rent that to someone else—maybe even to yourself!

Rating: 3/5

Change Accountants

Not all accountants are financially literate. You need to find the best accountant in your area. A really good tax and business accountant will cost you a lot of money but will also save you a lot.

Hints and Tips:

1. Choose an accountant who's always learning and increasing his skills.

2. Forget the diplomas on the wall. Ask questions and do some research on his past performance.

3. Remember, it's your money and he is working for *you*!

Rating: 5/5

Keep Overheads to a Minimum

The biggest killer of small business is signing long-term contracts that add to monthly fixed overheads. So many business owners think that payment over time will bring them success faster. Trust me, in a slow month the one thing you really don't want is fixed monthly costs. Aim to pay cash for as many larger purchases as you can, even if that means buying secondhand or waiting till you can afford it.

Hints and Tips:

1. Keep your fixed monthly expenses to a minimum.

2. Pay cash rather than lease.

Rating: 5/5

Stop Running Ads That Don't Work

If your ads aren't making you money, then stop running them. You should only run ads that make you money immediately. It is important to test and measure each ad to make sure that you're getting the maximum return possible. When you find one that works, keep using it.

Hints and Tips:

1. Constantly test and measure.

2. It doesn't matter whether you like it or not; if there isn't an immediate return on investment, dump it.

3. Keep experimenting until one really works, then keep running it.

Rating: 5/5

Regular/Timely Accounts

Send out seven-day accounts as soon as the job is completed, or the product has been delivered. Don't wait until the end of the month to send accounts out. The money is always better off in your account. Also, complete your monthly or weekly profit and loss report ASAP, so you know if you're making money.

Hints and Tips:

1. As soon as the sale is made, send out the account—better yet, get cash up-front.

2. If you are slack in sending out the account, customers will think it's OK for them to be slack in paying.

3. Don't leave it to chance. There should be systems that automate the whole process of sending out accounts and collecting money.

4. You cannot manage what you cannot measure, so complete monthly profit and loss reports within seven days of the end of the month.

Rating: 4/5

Get Your Bills Checked

Don't assume that your bills are correct. In many cases you can save money by checking them to find out if you've been overcharged. You must have someone check every bill, and then follow up any discrepancies.

Hints and Tips:

1. Take nothing for granted—always double-check every bill.

2. Keep all receipts and records of spending so you can cross-reference—you need to anyway for tax purposes.

3. There are computer programs out there that can check your bank loans. You'd be amazed how often people get overcharged by large institutions.

4. If you think there's a discrepancy, don't just shrug your shoulders. The amount(s)—sometimes with back interest—can really add up.

Rating: 4/5

Measure Everything

This needs to be applied to all areas of your business. Everything, from your advertising to the amount of phone calls you make, needs to be tested and measured. When you test and measure every area of your business, you can start to identify ways to cut costs and increase profits.

Hints and Tips:

1. Look at each area of your business individually.

2. Test and measure the response to every effort.

3. If you can't be objective enough yourself, get an outsider to take a look at things for you.

4. Constantly strive to make small improvements.

Rating: 5/5

YOUR FIVE KILLER PROFIT MARGIN STRATEGIES

It's now time for you to consider the proven ideas of increasing your profit margins and evaluating them in relation to your own particular situation. As with the other strategies, some will be more applicable than others..

Start by eliminating those that definitely won't suit your business. But before you do, think carefully. Can you adapt the idea to suit your situation? Identify the *five killer profit margin* strategies you think are most appropriate to your business right now.

Select the five you'd like to run with first and write the names of the strategies down on the form that follows. Next to each strategy fill in the date by which each is to be implemented.

Then add this page to those for the previous parts of the Business Chassis, and you'll have a workable, tried and tested *instant marketing plan* that will deliver results—guaranteed.

PROFIT MARGINS

Strategy 1: _____ Date: _____

Notes: _____
_____
_____
_____
_____

Strategy 2: _____ Date: _____

Notes: _____
_____
_____
_____
_____

Strategy 3: _____ Date: _____

Notes: _____
_____
_____
_____
_____

Strategy 4: _____ Date: _____

Notes: _____
_____
_____
_____
_____

Strategy 5: _____ Date: _____

Notes: _____
_____
_____
_____
_____

ACTION PLAN

Name of Strategy:

Type of Strategy: . . . .

Hard COSTS

Production $ . . . .

Envelopes $ . . . .

Paper $ . . . .

Printing $ . . . .

Postage $ . . . .

Advertising $ . . . .

Other $ . . . .

1. **Total Fixed Costs** $ . . . .

2. **Average $$$ Sale** $ . . . .

Variable COSTS

Telephone $ . . . .

Wages $ . . . .

Electricity $ . . . .

Rent $ . . . .

Brochure $ . . . .

Other Postage $ . . . .

Other $ . . . .

3. **Total Variables** $ . . . .

Delivery COSTS

Cost of Goods Sold $ . . . .

Taxes $ . . . .

Transportation $ . . . .

Packaging $ . . . .

Other $ . . . .

4. **Total Delivery** $ . . . .

5. **Net Profit [2/(3+4)]** $ . . . .

6. **Response Needed**

To Break Even (1/5) $ . . . .

Is This Strategy   Affordable ☐

Targeted ☐

Profitable ☐

Easy ☐

Proceed . . . .
(yes/no)? . . . .
. . . .
. . . .

Priority . . . .
(high/medium/low)? . . . .
. . . .
. . . .

Date to Start?
Commitment Made in Diary ☐

Feedback Gathered from Others ☐

Notes Made and Filed ☐

Extra Comments Below:

. . . .

. . . .

. . . .

. . . .

. . . .

. . . .

. . . .

. . . .

. . . .

. . . .

. . . .

. . . .

▌Testing and Measuring

Once again, I'm going to say it: Test and measure everything. Make it part of your daily business routine. And I know most businesspeople hate doing it. This is because it means there is a chance, however remote, that every marketing strategy they try will not work the first time. In other words, it is possible that they'll have to spend money without seeing any returns.

That makes this business of testing and measuring pretty unattractive to most people.

But consider this: You've probably been testing and measuring all your business life. Remember the newspaper advertising you tried that didn't work, and the radio spots that did OK?

That's all testing is.

The next step is to do it properly. Here are the six steps to successfully work out what *works*, what *has a chance*, and what *doesn't have a hope*.

STEP ONE

Start asking people where they heard about you. Start right now, immediately. If there's one thing I stress to business owners when consulting with them, it's this: If you don't know what's working and what's not, you can't possibly make informed decisions.

And you'll never know which ads to run. You may keep running an ad that never brings in a sale. It may also accidentally kill a good sale. Customers usually come from so many different sources that it's impossible to judge how an ad is working on sales alone. Perhaps you received more referrals that week, or there might have been a festival in town.

You need to find out for sure. Use the leads survey form or something similar and include all the ways people could hear about you: newspaper ads, direct mail, Yellow Pages, referrals, walk-bys, to mention but a few.

Every time someone buys, ask them this question: "By the way, can I just ask where you heard about my business?" No one, and I mean no one, will have any problem telling you. Make a mark on your your tally sheet in the relevant column. Keep track and ensure that every member of your team does the same. At the end of 14 or 28 days, tally up and get the figures.

Now you can start making decisions.

STEP TWO

Prune, modify, and increase.

The first thing to do is to identify what's not working. If your ad is getting a very low response (which means the profit margin from the sales is not at least paying for the ad), kill it right away. Of course, you do need to consider the lifetime value of the customers as well. If, after taking all factors into account, you're not getting results, bite the bullet and stop running it. Every time you do run it, you're giving away money.

Now you have two options: Channel your marketing funds elsewhere (like back into your pocket), or improve the ad.

If you choose option two, there are a couple of things you could do to make things simpler. First, go back over your past ads and think about how well each one worked. Pull out the best couple and see if you can pick what gave them the edge. Next, read my book *Instant Advertising*. Or at least thumb through it. And last, look at what your competitors are doing. Do they have an ad that they run every week? Unless they're stupid, the ad must be doing OK. What ideas can you glean from it?

Once you have done all this, sit down and write a new ad. Don't do anything with it yet—we'll get to that in a minute.

Go through this process with each marketing piece that doesn't seem to be working. Kill, examine, modify. Kill, examine, modify. Once you have a collection of these modified pieces, just sit on them—there's something more important you need to deal with first—the strategies that are working.

And always remember, the true test of a marketing strategy is whether it pays for itself. If you run an ad and it costs you $600 and makes you $1300 in profit, it's a good ad.

Run through each of the working strategies in depth, examining why they are producing results and the others aren't. See if you can pick the one attractive important point about each. This in itself will teach you a substantial amount about your business.

Next, think of a way to do each strategy on a larger scale. If it's flyers, the answer is simple: Drop twice as many flyers. That should bring twice the sales. If it's an ad, run it in more papers, or increase its size. If it's Yellow Pages, book a bigger space next time.

But whatever you do, don't meddle. Just do the same thing on a larger scale.

STEP THREE

Test and measure for another two weeks.

Notice if the number of inquiries remains the same, goes up, or goes down. Also compare this with how much you're spending on marketing.

You'll probably find that you hardly miss those dud strategies and that the larger-scale working strategies are paying off very nicely indeed. If they are not, return to the original or smaller size.

STEP FOUR

Check your conversion.

Conversion is a term that relates to the number of inquiries that become sales. You may find you get 1 in 10, 99 out of 100, or anything in between.

So many times when analyzing a business, I discover that poor marketing is not the problem. It's inadequate sales techniques. There are tons of businesses that have ample leads but insufficient skills to convert them into sales.

Be honest with yourself: What is your ratio of leads to sales? Is it possible to increase this ratio, even just a little?

In almost every case, it is. It simply requires a better understanding of the sales process and of the customers' needs. "But I'm a good salesperson; the other guys just beat me on price," is a common defense.

And while I wouldn't dispute this, I'm usually quick to point out that they're probably not giving the customer sufficient reason to buy from them in the first place. If you can get exactly the same thing elsewhere, and get it for less, you probably will.

But what if the salespeople at the more expensive shop actually took an interest in your needs? And what if they were a little bit friendlier? And what if they were willing to back their product with a guarantee? And what if they offered free delivery? All of these *what ifs* add up and can tip the scale.

STEP FIVE

Consolidate.

Leave it for a month or so, and work on converting the supply of leads you have. A better conversion technique, plus more leads from bigger-scale marketing strategies, should give your business a boost.

The lack of dead money being poured into ads that don't work should also give you a helping hand.

STEP SIX

Branch out.

Now it's time to implement some of the strategies you've chosen as part of your 25 killer marketing strategies. Do one at a time and track the results meticulously. Begin with those designed to generate leads. Note down exactly how many leads they bring you, and how many of those turn into sales. Compare that with your marketing costs and judge whether it has been a good strategy.

If so, add it to your list of ongoing strategies. If not, don't give up hope. Try again. Change it slightly. Change the headline or the medium. Amend the offer. Change a meaningful part of it and measure the results.

If it doesn't work again, give it another try, then another. If, after some time, you get the feeling nothing is going to work, abandon the idea and concentrate your efforts on another idea.

Very soon, you'll develop a collection of marketing strategies that work, and you'll have weeded out all the costly ones. Now that's a business success formula.

Success

You need to understand what success is before you know you've achieved it. This isn't fluffy stuff—this is about knowing when you've been successful and when you haven't.

For example, sometimes businesses will get hundreds of calls from people who want to take up a below-cost *loss-leader* deal. They all buy, but none ever comes back. The strategy got a high response, yet the business lost money.

Sometimes a classified ad will get hardly any calls, but every caller might buy, and buy a *lot*. Then, to make things even better, these customers may turn out to be loyal and come back every month. The strategy gets a low response, but the business makes a killing from such a small investment.

You'll be able to easily work out whether you've been successful by using the *Action Plans* included at the end of Part 4. But before you run any strategy, you should run through the following three-step process:

1. Work out your costs. This includes the cost of advertising, staff, phone calls, and offers.

2. Know your margins. You need to know the net profit you make from anyone who buys your product or service. By understanding how much you actually make from each sale, you'll be able to work out the percentage response required.

3. Lifetime value. Don't view each new customer as a one-time sale. You will normally lose money on the first sale to a new client. The average business will need to sell to a client 2-1/2 times before it begins to make a profit from her.

Forget about response rate—it's largely irrelevant. Here's an example that shows why: Let's say it costs 40 cents to contact each prospect. Let's also imagine that the product you're selling is priced at $23,000 and has a margin of 40 percent. You'd have to be pretty happy with a 1 percent conversion rate, wouldn't you? That means for every $9200 you earn, you have to spend $40. That's a pretty good return on investment. At the end of the day, that's all that matters.

Support

Are your team members ready to implement new ideas and support them? It's important that they understand the vital role they are about to play in every strategy. If your new customers come in and find your team is uninterested in giving them service, the exercise will be a waste of time.

Your team members also need to be shown how to work the strategy. They may also need lots of patience. It'll represent a new way of going about things, so give them time to adjust.

▋ Getting into *Action*

So, when is the best time to start?

Now—right now—so let me give you a step-by-step method to get yourself onto the same success path of many of my clients and the clients of my team at *Action International*.

Start testing and measuring now.

You'll want to ask your customers and prospects how they found out about you and your business. This will give you an idea of what's been working and what hasn't. You also want to concentrate on the five areas of the business chassis. Remember:

1. Number of Leads from each campaign.
2. Conversion Rate from each and every campaign.
3. Number of Transactions on average per year per customer.
4. Average Dollar Sale from each campaign.
5. Your Margins on each product or service.

The Number of Leads is easy; just take a measure for four weeks, average it out, and multiply by 50 working weeks of the year. Of course you'd ask each lead where they came from so you've got enough information to make advertising decisions.

The Conversion Rate is a little trickier, not because it's hard to measure, but because we want to know a few more details. You want to know what level of conversion you have from each and every type of marketing strategy you use. Remember that some customers won't buy right away, so keep accurate records on each and every lead.

To find the Number of Transactions you'll need to go through your records. Hopefully you can find the transaction history of at least 50 of your past customers and then average out their yearly purchases.

The Average Dollar Sale is as simple as it sounds. The total dollars sold divided by the number of sales. The best information you can collect is the average from each marketing campaign you run, so that you know where the real profit is coming from.

And, of course, your margins. An Average Margin is good to know and measure, but to know the margins on everything you sell is the most powerful knowledge you can collect.

If you're having any challenges with your testing and measuring, be sure to contact your nearest *Action International* Business Coach. She'll be able to help you through and show you the specialized documents to use.

If, by chance, you're thinking of racing ahead before you test and measure, remember this. It's impossible to improve a score when you don't know what the score is.

So you've got your starting point. You know exactly what's going on in your business right now. In fact, you know more about not only what's happening right now, but also the factors that are going to create what will happen tomorrow.

The next step in your business growth is simple.

Let's decide what you want out of the business—in other words, your goals. Here are the main points I want you to plan for.

How many hours do you want to work each week? How much money do you want to take out of the business each month? And, most importantly, when do you want to finish the business?

By "finish" the business, I mean when it will be systematized enough so it can run without your having to be there. Remember this about business; a little bit of planning goes a long way, but to make a plan you have to have a destination.

Once again, if you're having difficulty, talk to an *Action International* Business Coach. He'll know exactly how to help you find what it is you really want out of both your business and your life.

Now the real work begins.

Remember, our goal is to get a 10 percent increase in each area over the next 12 months. Choose well, but I want to warn you of one thing, one thing I can literally guarantee.

Eight out of 10 marketing campaigns you run *will not work.*

That's why when you choose to run, say, an advertising campaign in your local newspaper, you've got to run at least 10 different ads. When you select a direct mail campaign, you should send out at least 10 different letters to test, and so on.

Make sure you get at least five strategies under each heading and plan to run at least one, preferably two, at least each month for the next 12 months.

Don't work on just one of the five areas at a time; mix it up a little so you get the synergy of all five areas working together.

Now, this is the most important advice I can give you:

Learn how to make each and every strategy work. Don't just think you know what to do; go through my hints and tips, read more books, listen to as many tapes as you can, watch all the videos you can find, talk to the experts, and make sure you get the most advantage you can before you invest a whole lot of money.

The next 12 months are going to be a matter of doing the numbers, running the campaigns, testing headlines, testing offers, testing prices, and, of course, measuring the results.

By the end of it you should have at least five new strategies in each of the five areas working together to produce a great result.

Once again I want to stress that this will work and this will make your business grow as long as *you* work it.

Is it simple? *Yes.*

Is it easy? *No.*

You'll have to work hard. If you can get the guidance of someone who's been there before you, then get it.

Whatever you do, start it now, start it today, and most importantly, make the most of every day. Your past does not equal your future; you decide your future right here and right now.

Getting into *Action*

Be who you want to be, *do* what you need to do, in order to *have* what you want to have.

Positive *thought* without positive *Action* leaves you with positively *nothing*. I called my company *Action International,* not Theory International, or Yeah, I read that book International, but *Action International.*

So take the first step—and get into *Action.*

■ ABOUT THE AUTHOR

Bradley J. Sugars

Brad Sugars is a world-renowned Australian entrepreneur, author, and business coach who has helped more than a million clients around the world find business and personal success.

He's a trained accountant, but as he puts it, most of his experience comes from owning his own companies. Brad's been in business for himself since age 15 in some way or another, although his father would argue he started at 7 when he was caught selling his Christmas presents to his brothers. He's owned and operated more than two dozen companies, from pizza to ladies fashion, from real estate to insurance and many more.

His main company, *Action International*, started from humble beginnings in the back bedroom of a suburban home in 1993 when Brad started teaching business owners how to grow their sales and marketing results. Now *Action* has nearly 1000 franchises in 19 countries and is ranked in the top 100 franchises in the world.

Brad Sugars has spoken on stage with the likes of Tom Hopkins, Brian Tracy, John Maxwell, Robert Kiyosaki, and Allen Pease, written books with people like Anthony Robbins, Jim Rohn, and Mark Victor Hansen, appeared on countless TV and radio programs and in literally hundreds of print articles around the globe. He's been voted as one of the Most Admired Entrepreneurs by the readers of *E-Spy* magazine—next to the likes of Rupert Murdoch, Henry Ford, Richard Branson, and Anita Roddick.

Today, *Action International* has coaches across the globe and is ranked as one of the Top 25 Fastest Growing Franchises on the planet as well as the #1 Business Consulting Franchise. The success of *Action International* is simply attributed to the fact that they apply the strategies their coaches use with business owners.

Brad is a proud father and husband, the chairman of a major children's charity and in his own words, "a very average golfer."

Check out Brad's Web site www.bradsugars.com and read the literally hundreds of testimonials from those who've gone before you.

■ RECOMMENDED READING LIST

ACTION INTERNATIONAL BOOK LIST

"The only difference between *you* now and *you* in 5 years' time will be the people you meet and the books you read." Charlie Tremendous Jones

"And, the only difference between *your* income now and *your* income in 5 years' time will be the people you meet, the books you read, the tapes you listen to, and then how *you* apply it all." Brad Sugars

- *The E-Myth Revisited* by Michael E. Gerber
- *My Life in Advertising & Scientific Advertising* by Claude Hopkins
- *Tested Advertising Methods* by John Caples
- *Building the Happiness Centered Business* by Dr. Paddi Lund
- *Write Language* by Paul Dunn & Alan Pease
- *7 Habits of Highly Effective People* by Steven Covey
- *First Things First* by Steven Covey
- *Awaken the Giant Within* by Anthony Robbins
- *Unlimited Power* by Anthony Robbins
- *22 Immutable Laws of Marketing* by Al Ries & Jack Trout
- *21 Ways to Build a Referral Based Business* by Brad Sugars
- *21 Ways to Increase Your Advertising Response* by Mark Tier
- *The One Minute Salesperson* by Spencer Johnson & Larry Wilson
- *The One Minute Manager* by Spencer Johnson & Kenneth Blanchard
- *The Great Sales Book* by Jack Collis
- *Way of the Peaceful Warrior* by Dan Millman
- *How to Build a Championship Team*—Six Audio tapes by Blair Singer
- Brad Sugars "Introduction to Sales & Marketing" 3-hour Video
- Leverage—Board Game by Brad Sugars
- *17 Ways to Increase Your Business Profits* booklet & tape by Brad Sugars. FREE OF CHARGE to Business Owners

*To order Brad Sugars' products from the recommended reading list, call your nearest *Action International* office today.

■ The 18 Most Asked Questions about Working with an *Action International* Business Coach

And 18 great reasons why you'll jump at the chance to get your business flying and make your dreams come true

1. So who is *Action International?*

Action International is a business Coaching and Consulting company started in 1993 by entrepreneur and author Brad Sugars. With offices around the globe and business coaches from Singapore to Sydney to San Francisco, *Action International* has been set up with you, the business owner, in mind.

Unlike traditional consulting firms, *Action* is designed to give you both short-term assistance and long-term training through its affordable Mentoring approach. After 12 years teaching business owners how to succeed, *Action's* more than 10,000 clients and 1,000,000 seminar attendees will attest to the power of the programs.

Based on the sales, marketing, and business management systems created by Brad Sugars, your *Action* Coach is trained to not only show you how to increase your business revenues and profits, but also how to develop the business so that you as the owner work less and relax more.

Action International is a franchised company, so your local *Action* Coach is a fellow business owner who's invested her own time, money, and energy to make her business succeed. At *Action,* your success truly does determine our success.

2. And, why do I need a Business Coach?

Every great sports star, business person, and superstar is surrounded by coaches and advisors.

And, as the world of business moves faster and gets more competitive, it's difficult to keep up with both the changes in your industry and the innovations in sales, marketing, and management strategies. Having a business coach is no longer a luxury; it's become a necessity.

On top of all that, it's impossible to get an objective answer from yourself. Don't get me wrong. You can survive in business without the help of a Coach, but it's almost impossible to thrive.

A Coach *can* see the forest for the trees. A Coach will make you focus on the game. A Coach will make you run more laps than you feel like. A Coach will tell it like it is. A Coach will give you small pointers. A Coach will listen. A Coach will be your marketing manager, your sales director, your training coordinator, your partner, your confidant, your mentor, your best friend, and an *Action* Business Coach will help you make your dreams come true.

3. Then, what's an Alignment Consultation?

Great question. It's where an *Action* Coach starts with every business owner. You'll invest a minimum of $1295, and during the initial 2 to 3 hours your Coach invests with you, he'll learn as much as he can about your business, your goals, your challenges, your sales, your marketing, your finances, and so much more.

All with three goals in mind: To know exactly where your business is now. To clarify your goals both in the business and personally. And thirdly, to get the crucial pieces of information he needs to create your businesses *Action* Plan for the next 12 months.

Not a traditional business or marketing plan mind you, but a step-by-step plan of *Action* that you'll work through as you continue with the Mentor Program.

4. So, what, then, is the Mentor Program?

Simply put, it's where your *Action* Coach will work with you for a full 12 months to make your goals a reality. From weekly coaching calls and goal-setting sessions, to creating marketing pieces together, you will develop new sales strategies and business systems so you can work less and learn all that you need to know about how to make your dreams come true.

You'll invest between $995 and $10,000 a month and your Coach will dedicate a minimum of 5 hours a month to working with you on your sales, marketing, team building, business development, and every step of the *Action* Plan you created from your Alignment Consultation.

Unlike most consultants, your *Action* Coach will do more than just show you what to do. She'll be with you when you need her most, as each idea takes shape, as each campaign is put into place, as you need the little pointers on making it happen, when you need someone to talk to, when you're faced with challenges and, most importantly, when you're just not sure what to do next. Your Coach will be there every step of the way.

5. Why at least 12 months?

If you've been in business for more than a few weeks, you've seen at least one or two so called "quick fixes."

Most Consultants seem to think they can solve all your problems in a few hours or a few days. At *Action* we believe that long-term success means not just scraping the surface and doing it for you. It means doing it with you, showing you how to do it, working alongside you, and creating the success together.

Over the 12 months, you'll work on different areas of your business, and month by month you'll not only see your goals become a reality, you'll gain both the confidence and the knowledge to make it happen again and again, even when your first 12 months of Coaching is over.

6. How can you be sure this will work in my industry and in my business?

Very simple. You see at *Action,* we're experts in the areas of sales, marketing, business development, business management, and team building just to name a few. With 328 different profit-building strategies, you'll soon see just how powerful these systems are.

You, on the other hand, are the expert in your business and together we can apply the *Action* systems to make your business fly.

Add to this the fact that within the *Action* Team at least one of our Coaches has either worked with, managed, worked in, or even owned a business that's the same or very similar to yours. Your *Action* Coach has the full resources of the entire *Action* team to call upon for every challenge you have. Imagine hundreds of experts ready to help you.

7. Won't this just mean more work?

Of course when you set the plan with your *Action* Coach, it'll all seem like a massive amount of work, but no one ever said attaining your goals would be easy.

In the first few months, it'll take some work to adjust, some work to get over the hump so to speak. The further you are into the program, the less and less work you'll have to do.

You will, however, be literally amazed at how focused you'll be and how much you'll get done. With focus, an *Action* Coach, and most importantly the *Action* Systems, you'll be achieving a whole lot more with the same or even less work.

8. How will I find the time?

Once again the first few months will be the toughest, not because of an extra amount of work, but because of the different work. In fact, your *Action* Coach will show you how to, on a day-to-day basis, get more work done with less effort.

In other words, after the first few months you'll find that you're not working more, just working differently. Then, depending on your goals from about month six onwards, you'll start to see the results of all your work, and if you choose to, you can start working less than ever before. Just remember, it's about changing what you do with your time, *not* putting in more time.

9. How much will I need to invest?

Nothing, if you look at it from the same perspective as we do. That's the difference between a cost and an investment. Everything you do with your *Action* Coach is a true investment in your future.

Not only will you create great results in your business, but you'll end up with both an entrepreneurial education second to none, and the knowledge that you can repeat your successes over and over again.

As mentioned, you'll need to invest at least $1295 up to $5000 for the Alignment Consultation and Training Day, and then between $995 and $10,000 a month for the next 12 months of coaching.

Your Coach may also suggest several books, tapes, and videos to assist in your training, and yes, they'll add to your investment as you go. Why? Because having an *Action* Coach is just like having a marketing manager, a sales team leader, a trainer, a recruitment specialist, and corporate consultant all for half the price of a secretary.

10. Will it cost me extra to implement the strategies?

Once again, give your *Action* Coach just half an hour and he'll show you how to turn your marketing into an investment that yields sales and profits rather than just running up your expenses.

In most cases we'll actually save you money when we find the areas that aren't working for you. But yes, I'm sure you'll need to spend some money to make some money.

Yet, when you follow our simple testing and measuring systems, you'll never risk more than a few dollars on each campaign, and when we find the ones that work, we make sure you keep profiting from them time and again.

Remember, when you go the accounting way of saving costs, you can only ever add a few percent to the bottom line.

Following Brad Sugars' formula, your *Action* Coach will show you that through sales, marketing, and income growth, your possible returns are exponential.

The sky's the limit, as they say.

11. Are there any guarantees?

To put it bluntly, no. Your *Action* Coach will never promise any specific results, nor will she guarantee that any of your goals will become a reality.

You see, we're your coach. You're still the player, and it's up to you to take the field. Your Coach will push you, cajole you, help you, be there for you, and even do some things with you, but you've still got to do the work.

Only *you* can ever be truly accountable for your own success and at *Action* we know this to be a fact. We guarantee to give you the best service we can, to answer your questions promptly, and with the best available information. And, last but not least your *Action* Coach is committed to making you successful whether you like it or not.

That's right, once we've set the goals and made the plan, we'll do whatever it takes to make sure you reach for that goal and strive with all your might to achieve all that you desire.

Of course we'll be sure to keep you as balanced in your life as we can. We'll make sure you never compromise either the long-term health and success of your company or yourself, and more importantly your personal set of values and what's important to you.

12. What results have other business owners seen?

Anything from previously working 60 hours a week down to working just 10—right through to increases in revenues of 100s and even 1000s of percent. Results speak for themselves. Be sure to keep reading for specific examples of real people, with real businesses, getting real results.

There are three reasons why this will work for you in your business. Firstly, your *Action* Coach will help you get 100 percent focused on your goals and the step-by-step processes to get you there. This focus alone is amazing in its effect on you and your business results.

Secondly, your coach will hold you accountable to get things done, not just for the day-to-day running of the business, but for the dynamic growth of the business. You're investing in your success and we're going to get you there.

Thirdly, your Coach is going to teach you one-on-one as many of *Action's* 328 profit-building strategies as you need. So whether your goal is to be making more money, or working fewer hours or both inside the next 12 months your goals can become a reality. Just ask any of the thousands of existing *Action* clients, or more specifically, check out the results of 19 of our most recent clients shown later in this section.

13. What areas will you coach me in?

There are five main areas your *Action* Coach will work on with you. Of course, how much of each depends on you, your business, and your goals.

Sales. The backbone of creating a superprofitable business, and one area we'll help you get spectacular results in.

Marketing and Advertising. If you want to get a sale, you've got to get a prospect. Over the next 12 months your *Action* Coach will teach you Brad Sugars' amazingly simple streetwise marketing—marketing that makes profits.

Team Building and Recruitment. You'll never *wish* for the right people again. You'll have motivated and passionate team members when your Coach shows you how.

Systems and Business Development. Stop the business from running you and start running your business. Your Coach will show you the secrets to having the business work, even when you're not there.

Customer Service. How to deliver consistently, make it easy to buy, and leave your customers feeling delighted with your service. Both referrals and repeat business are centered in the strategies your Coach will teach you.

14. Can you also train my people?

Yes. We believe that training your people is almost as important as coaching you.

Your investment starts at $1500 for your entire team, and you can decide between five very powerful in-house training programs. From "*Sales Made Simple*" for your face-to-face sales team to "*Phone Power*" for your entire team's telephone etiquette and sales ability. Then you can run the "*Raving Fans*" customer service training or the "*Total Team*" training. And finally, if you're too busy earning a living to make any real money, then you've just got to attend our "*Business Academy 101.*" It will make a huge impact on your finances, business, career, family, and lifestyle. You'll be amazed at how much involvement and excitement comes out of your team with each training program.

15. Can you write ads, letters, and marketing pieces for me?

Yes. Your *Action* Coach can do it for you, he can train you to do it yourself, or we can simply critique the marketing pieces you're using right now.

If you want us to do it for you, our one-time fees start at just $1195. You'll not only get one piece; we'll design several pieces for you to take to the market and see which one performs the best. Then, if it's a critique you're after, just $349 means we'll work through your entire piece and give you feedback on what to change, how to change it, and what else you should do. Last but not least, for between $15 and $795 we can recommend a variety of books, tapes, and most importantly, Brad Sugars' Instant Success series books that'll take you step-by-step through the how-tos of creating your marketing pieces.

16. Why do you also recommend books, tapes, and videos?

Basically, to save you time and money. Take Brad Sugars' *Sales Rich* DVD or Video Series, for instance. In about 16 hours you'll learn more about business than you have in the last 12 years. It'll also mean your *Action* Coach works with you on the high-level implementation rather than the very basic teaching.

It's a very powerful way for you to speed up the coaching process and get phenomenal rather than just great results.

17. When is the best time to get started?

Yesterday. OK, seriously, right now, today, this minute, before you take another step, waste another dollar, lose another sale, work too many more hours, miss another family event, forget another special occasion.

Far too many business people wait and see. They think working harder will make it all better. Remember, what you know got you to where you are. To get to where you want to go, you've got to make some changes and most probably learn something new.

There's no time like the present to get started on your dreams and goals.

18. So how do we get started?

Well, you'd better get back in touch with your *Action* Coach. There's some very simple paperwork to sign, and then you're on your way.

You'll have to invest a few hours showing them everything about your business. Together you'll get a plan created and then the work starts. Remember, it may seem like a big job at the start, but with a Coach, you're sharing the load and together you'll achieve great things.

Here's what others say about what happened after working with an *Action* business coach

Paul and Rosemary Rose—Icontact Multimedia

"Our *Action* coach showed us several ways to help market our product. We went on to triple our client base and simultaneously tripled our profits in just seven months. It was unbelievable! Last year was our best Christmas ever. We were really able to spoil ourselves!"

S. Ford—Pride Kitchens

"In 6 months, I've gone from working more than 60 hours per week in my business to less than 20, and my conversion rate's up from 19 percent to 62 percent. I've now got some life back!"

Gary and Leanne Paper—Galea Timber Products

"We achieved our goal for the 12 months within a 6-month period with a 100 percent increase in turnover and a good increase in margins. We have already recommended and will continue to recommend this program to others."

Russell, Kevin, John, and Karen—Northern Lights Power and Distribution

"Our profit margin has increased from 8 percent to 21 percent in the last 8 months. *Action* coaching focussed us on what are our most profitable markets."

Ty Pedersen—De Vries Marketing Sydney

"After just three months of coaching, my sales team's conversion rate has grown from an average of less than 12 percent to more than 23 percent and our profits have climbed by more than 30 percent."

Hank Meerkerk and Hemi McGarvey—B.O.P. School of Welding

"Last year we started off with a profit forecast, but as soon as we got *Action* involved we decided to double our forecast. We're already well over that forecast again by two-and-a-half times on turnover, and profits are even higher. Now we run a really profitable business."

Stuart Birch—Education Personnel Limited

"One direct mail letter added $40,000 to my bottom line, and working with *Action* has given me quality time to work on my business and spend time with my family."

Mark West—Wests Pumping and Irrigation

"In four months two simple strategies have increased our business more than 20 percent. We're so busy, we've had to delay expanding the business while we catch up!"

Michael Griffiths—Gym Owner

"I went from working 70 hours per week *in* the business to just 25 hours, with the rest of the time spent working *on* the business."

Cheryl Standring—In Harmony Landscapes

"We tried our own direct mail and only got a 1 percent response. With *Action* our response rate increased to 20 percent. It's definitely worth every dollar we've invested."

Jason and Chris Houston—Empradoor Finishing

"After 11 months of working with *Action,* we have increased our sales by 497 percent, and the team is working without our having to be there."

Michael Avery—Coomera Pet Motels

"I was skeptical at first, but I knew we needed major changes in our business. In 2 months, our extra profits were easily covering our investment and our predictions for the next 10 months are amazing."

Garry Norris—North Tax & Accounting

"As an accountant, my training enables me to help other business people make more money. It is therefore refreshing when someone else can help me do the same. I have a policy of only referring my clients to people who are professional, good at what they do, and who have personally given me great service. *Action* fits all three of these criteria, and I recommend *Action* to my business clients who want to grow and develop their businesses further."

Lisa Davis and Steve Groves—Mt. Eden Motorcycles

"With *Action* we increased our database from 800 to 1200 in 3 months. We consistently get about 20 new qualified people on our database each week for less than $10 per week."

Christine Pryor—U-Name-It Embroidery

"Sales for August this year have increased 352 percent. We're now targeting a different market and we're a lot more confident about what we're doing."

Joseph Saitta and Michelle Fisher—Banyule Electrics

"Working with *Action,* our inquiry rate has doubled. In four months our business has changed so much our customers love us. It's a better place for people to work and our margins are widening."

Kevin and Alison Snook—Property Sales

"In the 12 months previous to working with *Action,* we had sold one home in our subdivision. In the first eight months of working with *Action,* we sold six homes. The results speak for themselves."

Wayne Manson—Hospital Supplies

"When I first looked at the Mentoring Program it looked expensive, but from the inside looking out, its been the best money I have ever spent. Sales are up more than $3000 per month since I started, and the things I have learned and expect to learn will ensure that I will enjoy strong sustainable growth in the future."

■ *Action* Contact Details

Action International Asia Pacific

Ground Floor, *Action* House, 2 Mayneview Street, Milton QLD 4064

Ph: +61 (0) 7 3368 2525

Fax: +61 (0) 7 3368 2535

Free Call: 1800 670 335

Action International Europe

Olympic House, Harbor Road, Howth, Co. Dublin, Ireland

Ph: +353 (0) 1-832 0213

Fax: +353 (0) 1-839 4934

Action International North America

5670 Wynn Road Suite A & C, Las Vegas, Nevada 89118

Ph: +1 (702) 795 3188

Fax: +1 (702) 795 3183

Free Call: (888) 483 2828

Action International UK

3–5 Richmond Hill, Richmond, Surrey, TW 106RE

Ph: +44 020 8948 5151

Fax: +44 020 8948 4111

Action Offices around the globe:

Australia | Canada | China | England | France | Germany | Hong Kong

India | Indonesia | Ireland | Malaysia | Mexico | New Zealand

Phillippines | Scotland | Spain | Singapore | USA | Wales

Here's how you can profit from all of Brad's ideas with your local *Action International* **Business Coach**

Just like a sporting coach pushes an athlete to achieve optimum performance, provides them with support when they are exhausted, and teaches the athlete to execute plays that the competition does not anticipate.

A business coach will make you run more laps than you feel like. A business coach will show it like it is. And a business coach will listen.

The role of an *Action* Business Coach is to show you how to improve your business through guidance, support, and encouragement. Your coach will help you with your sales, marketing, management, team building, and so much more. Just like a sporting coach, your *Action* Business Coach will help you and your business perform at levels you never thought possible.

Whether you've been in business for a week or 20 years, it's the right time to meet with and see how you'll profit from an *Action* Coach.

As the owner of a business it's hard enough to keep pace with all the changes and innovations going on in your industry, let alone to find the time to devote to sales, marketing, systems, planning and team management, and then to run your business as well.

As the world of business moves faster and becomes more competitive, having a Business Coach is no longer a luxury; it has become a necessity. Based on the sales, marketing, and business management systems created by Brad Sugars, your *Action* Coach is trained to not only show you how to increase your business revenues and profits but also how to develop your business so that you, as the owner, can take back control. All with the aim of your working less and relaxing more. Making money is one thing; having the time to enjoy it is another.

Your *Action* Business Coach will become your marketing manager, your sales director, your training coordinator, your confidant, your mentor. In short, your *Action* Coach will help you make your business dreams come true.

ATTENTION BUSINESS OWNERS
You can increase your profits now

Here's how you can have one of Brad's *Action* *International* Business Coaches guide you to success.

Like every successful sporting icon or team, a business needs a coach to help it achieve its full potential. In order to guarantee your business success, you can have one of Brad's team as your business coach. You will learn about how you can get amazing results with the help of the team at *Action* *International*.

The business coaches are ready to take you and your business on a journey that will reward you for the rest of your life. You see, we believe *Action* speaks louder than words.

Complete and post this card to your local *Action* office to discover how our team can help you increase your income today!

Action *International*

The World's Number-1 Business Coaching Team

Name ....

Position ....

Company ....

Address ....

....

Country ....

Phone ....

Fax ....

Email ....

Referred by ....

How do I become an *Action* International **Business Coach?**

If you choose to invest your time and money in a great business and you're looking for a white-collar franchise opportunity to build yourself a lifestyle, an income, a way to take control of your life and, a way to get great personal satisfaction …

Then you've just found the world's best team!

Now, it's about finding out if you've got what it takes to really enjoy and thrive in this amazing business opportunity.

Here are the 4 things we look for in every *Action* Coach:

1. You've got to love succeeding

We're looking for people who love success, who love getting out there and making things happen. People who enjoy mixing with other people, people who thrive on learning and growing, and people who want to charge an hourly rate most professionals only dream of.

2. You've got to love being in charge of your own life

When you're ready to take control, the key is to be in business for yourself, but not by yourself. *Action*'s support, our training, our world leading systems, and the backup of a global team are all waiting to give you the best chance of being an amazing business success.

3. You've got to love helping people

Being a great Coach is all about helping yourself by helping others. The first time clients thank you for showing them step by step how to make more money and work less within their business, will be the day you realize just how great being an *Action* Business Coach really is.

4. You've got to love a great lifestyle

Working from home, setting your own timetable, spending time with family and friends, knowing that the hard work you do is for your own company and, not having to climb a so-called corporate ladder. This is what lifestyle is all about. Remember, business is supposed to give you a life, not take it away.

Our business is booming and we're seriously looking for people ready to find out more about how becoming a member of the *Action* International Business Coaching team is going to be the best decision you've ever made.

Apply online now at www.action-international.com

Here's how you can network, get new leads, build yourself an instant sales team, learn, grow and build a great team of supportive business owners around you by checking into your local *Action* Profit Club

Joining your local *Action* Profit Club is about more than just networking, it's also the learning and exchanging of profitable ideas.

Embark on a journey to a more profitable enterprise by meeting with fellow, like-minded business owners.

An ***Action*** Profit Club is an excellent way to network with business people and business owners. You will meet every two weeks for breakfast to network and learn profitable strategies to grow your business.

Here are three reasons why ***Action*** *International's* Profit Clubs work where other networking groups don't:

1. You know networking is a great idea. The challenge is finding the time and maintaining the motivation to keep it up and make it a part of your business. If you're not really having fun and getting the benefits, you'll find it gets easier to find excuses that stop you going. So, we guarantee you will always have fun and learn a lot from your bi-weekly group meetings.
2. The real problem is that so few people do any work 'on' their business. Instead they generally work "in" it, until it's too late. By being a member of an ***Action*** Profit Club, you get to attend FREE business-building workshops run by Business Coaches that teach you how to work "on" your business and avoid this common pitfall and help you to grow your business.
3. Unlike other groups, we have marketing systems to assist in your groups' growth rather than just relying on you to bring in new members. This way you can concentrate on YOUR business rather than on ours.

Latest statistics show that the average person knows at least 200 other contacts. By being a member of your local ***Action*** Profit Club, you have an instant network of around 3,000 people

Join your local *Action* Profit Club today.

Apply online now at www.actionprofitclub.com

LEVERAGE—The Game of Business
Your Business Success is just a Few Games Away

Leverage—The Game of Business is a fun way to learn how to succeed in business fast.

The rewards start flowing the moment you start playing!

Leverage is three hours of fun, learning, and discovering how you can be an amazingly successful business person.

It's a breakthrough in education that will have you racking up the profits in no time. The principles you take away from playing this game will set you up for a life of business success. It will open your mind to what's truly possible. Apply what you learn and **sit back and watch your profits soar.**

By playing this fun and interactive business game, you will learn:

- How to quickly raise your business income
- How business people can become rich and successful in a short space of time
- How to create a business that works without you

Isn't it time you had the edge over your competition?

Leverage has been played by all age groups from 12-85 and has been a huge learning experience for all. The most common comment we hear is: 'I thought I knew a lot, and just by playing a simple board game I have realized I have a long way to go. The knowledge I've gained from playing Leverage will make me thousands! Thanks for the lesson.'

To order your copy online today, please visit www.bradsugars.com

Also available in the

THE BUSINESS COACH

Learn how to master the six steps on
the ladder of success

(0-07-146672-X)

INSTANT REPEAT BUSINESS

Build a solid and loyal
customer base

(0-07-146666-5)

THE REAL ESTATE COACH

Invest in real estate with
little or no cash

(0-07-146662-2)

INSTANT SALES

Master the crucial first minute of
any sales call

(0-07-146664-9)

INSTANT PROMOTIONS

Create powerful press releases, amazing
ads, and brilliant brochures

(0-07-146665-7)

INSTANT
SUCCESS
Real Results. Right Now.

Instant Success series.

INSTANT CASHFLOW
Turn every lead into a sale

(0-07-146659-2)

BILLIONAIRE IN TRAINING
Learn the wealth building secrets
of billionaires

(0-07-146661-4)

INSTANT PROFIT
Boost your bottom line with
a cash-building plan

(0-07-146668-1)

SUCCESSFUL FRANCHISING
Learn how to buy or sell a franchise

(0-07-146671-1)

INSTANT ADVERTISING
Create ads that stand out and sell

(0-07-146660-6)

INSTANT REFERRALS
Never cold call or chase after
customers again

(0-07-146667-3)

INSTANT LEADS
Generate a steady flow of leads

(0-07-146663-0)

INSTANT SYSTEMS
Stop running your business and start
growing it

(0-07-146670-3)

INSTANT TEAM BUILDING
Learn the six keys to a winning team

(0-07-146669-X)

*Your source for the strategies, skills,
and confidence every business owner
needs to succeed.*